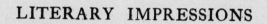

LITERARY IMPRESSIONS

Literary Impressions

BY
JULES LEMAÎTRE

TRANSLATED BY
A. W. EVANS

KENNIKAT PRESS
Port Washington, N. Y./London

LITERARY IMPRESSIONS

First published in 1921
Reissued in 1971 by Kennikat Press
Library of Congress Catalog Card No: 77-105801
ISBN 0-8046-1360-5

Manufactured by Taylor Publishing Company   Dallas, Texas

CONTENTS

INTRODUCTION

' THE good critic,' says Anatole France, ' is he who relates the adventures of his own soul among masterpieces.' The sentence might be printed as a motto on each of the eight volumes of M. Jules Lemaître's *Les Contemporains*, from which the essays in this book have been selected. For no writer, except Anatole France himself, was a more successful practitioner of personal and impressionist criticism than M. Jules Lemaître. If in the confrontation of forces caused, or rather made evident, by the Dreyfus affair, the two men found themselves in opposite camps, and if afterwards they receded farther from one another rather than drew closer together, there are striking fundamental resemblances between them. Jules Lemaître's scepticism was never so profound as that of Anatole France, nor was his irony so deep-seated and universal, but the readers of Anatole France will recognize in Lemaître the same supple, sympathetic, irreverent, melancholy-humorous, questing and tasting mind. What pleases us in both is that their writings, and especially their critical writings, reflect the soul and spirit of the author, and that for both of them criticism is the art of enjoying books by showing them to us as seen through a temperament.

It is perhaps in the famous controversy with Brunetière, which added so greatly to the gaiety of letters, that one sees what a large fund of ideas Anatole France and Jules Lemaître held in common, at any rate at one period in the lives of both. Brunetière threw himself into the dispute with special ardour, feeling that the very foundations of his critical creed were at stake. But all his erudition and acuteness were ably countered by the not inferior erudition and the daring irreverence of his opponents. To Brunetière's almost pathetic assertions that criticism to be of any value must be ' objective,' that the difference between a good work of art and a bad one could only be determined by reason and comparison, and that the critic must go by fixed standards, Anâtole France replied by denying the possibility of 'objective' criticism, smiling at reason, and flouting the fixity of any such critical standards. Jules Lemaître, in a tone of bantering reverence, admitted that he was a sinner, and extended his respectful sympathy to Brunetière, the saint.

' M. Brunetière is incapable, it seems to me, of considering any work, whatever it be, great or small, except in its relations with a group of other works, whose relations with other groups, throughout time and space, are immediately evident to him ; and so on. A whole philosophy of literary history and at the same time a whole system of æsthetics and a whole system of ethics are visibly implied in the least of his judgments. Marvellous gift ! When he is reading a book, he is thinking, one may say, of all the books that have been written since the beginning of the world. He touches nothing which he does not class, and that for eternity. I admire the majesty of such criticism. . . . But look at what it costs. How sad it must be not to be able to open a book without remembering others and without comparing it with them! To judge always is perhaps never to enjoy. I should not be astonished if M. Brunetière had become really incapable of " reading for his own pleasure." He would be afraid of being a dupe, he would even be afraid of committing a sin. For us, it matters not if we make a mistake in liking what pleases us or amuses us, or if we have to smile to-morrow at our admirations of to-day. Our errors are without consequence ; they are not bound up with one another ; they only concern particular cases. If M. Brunetière, on the other hand, made a mistake, it would be frightful ; for besides the fact that he would have had no pleasure in his error, it would be without help or remedy ; it would be total and irreparable ; it would be the wreck of his whole being.'

Having thus shown the disadvantages inherent in Brunetière's method, Lemaître expounded the advantages of his own. That method he asserted is simply to define and explain the impressions that he received from works of art. This is a modest pretension, but it has its uses. It is impossible, for example, to give the reasons why one has received an impression from a work of art without dealing with general ideas, and distinguishing one's particular impression from the whole order of general impressions. Hence, the impressionist critic, while apparently only describing feeling aroused in his own mind, is really making himself the interpreter of a whole class of minds that are like his own. And what, after all, are literary doctrines but disguised preferences? He agreed with Anatole France that criticism is a sort of romance intended for those who have sagacious and curious minds, and that every romance is, in the last resort, an autobiography, and he added (in his estimate of that most systematic of thinkers, Taine) that all philosophy is in its essence poetry.

When the impressionist critic has thus expounded his doctrine of universal relativity and has explained that, as he is imprisoned in his own personality, there is no standard to which he may refer his own opinions or those of others, he may be asked to state what then is the value of criticism. To this M. Lemaître replied that to become acquainted with the sensations aroused in another personality by reading a book that pleases is to prolong and intensify our own sensations. And it does even more. As personalities differ, so every reader understands a work of art in his own way and according to his own nature. A critic is struck by some special aspect of the work he is studying, and he brings this special aspect into prominence, thus enabling his readers to see and enjoy something to which they might otherwise have been blind. In this way he collaborates with the artist whose work he considers, and he sometimes improves upon it ; for ' literary criticism can be an exquisite thing, and can equal or even surpass in interest the very works that occupy it. . . . To the ancient definition, *Arshomo additus naturæ*, one might add, *Critica scriptor additus scriptori*, or something approaching it.'

Thus professing no doctrine, M. Lemaître had no temptation to conceal his doubts and contradictions. These the dogmatic critic must needs keep from his readers, or confess his own incapacity. But M. Lemaître's sincerity is proved by the unpleasant things which he sometimes said to his friends. This is the price he felt compelled to pay for his freedom from system, and to those who reproached him for analysing his impressions instead of judging works and basing his judgments on general principles of æsthetics, he replied :

'I assure you, it is possible for me, as for other people, to judge on principles and not on impressions. Only if I did so I should not be sincere. I should say things of which I should not be sure, whilst I am sure of my impressions. I can, on the whole, only describe myself in my contact with the works that are submitted to me. That can be done without indiscretion or self-conceit, for there is a part of our personality in each of us which can interest everybody. You say this is not criticism ? Then it is something else, and I am not greatly concerned about the name you give to what I write.'

Of course a great deal depends on the
personality which the critic describes in its
contact with works of art, and in this respect
M. Lemaître has at all events succeeded in
interesting an immense number of readers.
From the moment when the essays that have
been collected in *Les Contemporains* began to
appear in the *Revue Bleue* he was recognized as one of the most brilliant of French
critics. How far the distinction of this
'Renan of reviewers,' as he has been called,
is due to his admirable style, is a matter on
which a foreigner must be slow to give an
opinion. One can, however, quote the opinions
of two of Júles Lemaître's fellow-countrymen
whose views are entitled to carry weight. 'No
one writes better than he does,' said his old
opponent, Brunetière, ' or in a more vivid,
more supple, or less commonplace style ; he
plays with words, he does as he wishes with
them, he juggles with them.' [1] And M. Victor
Giraud claims that Lemaître's style is more
natural, and smacks less of the lamp than even
the style of Anatole France.[2] It does not

[1] *Essais sur la Littérature Contemporaine*, p. 3.
[2] *Les Maîtres de l'Heure*, vol. ii., p. 36.

require more than a moderate knowledge of his language to see that, whatever else he is, he is a born writer, a bold as well as a skilful master of words.

It may be added that these essays were translated during M. Lemaître's lifetime, and that they are now published, not only as examples of his manner and method, but as embodying the views of a leader of French literature during a period which has now passed and from which the war has increased our sense of separation. Possibly this latter fact may give them an added interest for English readers.

LITERARY IMPRESSIONS

ANATOLE FRANCE

Can it be possible that I very nearly blamed M. Weiss for being an unstable and capricious critic and for not having a yard-measure in his pocket by which to measure the works of the mind? One of Montaigne's favourite thoughts is that we can have no certain knowledge since nothing is immutable, neither things nor intelligences, and the mind and its object are both borne along in perpetual movement. Ourselves changing, we behold a changing world. And even when the object under observation is for ever fixed in its forms, the mind in which it is reflected is mutable and multifarious, and this is enough to make it impossible for us to be responsible for anything more than our momentary impression.

How, therefore, could literary criticism constitute itself into a doctrine? Works pass in procession before the mirror of our minds;

but, as the procession is long, the mirror becomes modified in the interval, and when by chance the same work returns, it no longer projects tne same image.

Any one can try the experiment on himself. I have adored Corneille, and I have been within an ace of despising Racine : at the present moment I adore Corneille, and Racine is almost indifferent to me. The transports into which Musset's verses used to throw me, I can recapture now no longer. I have lived with my ears and eyes filled by Victor Hugo's resonance and enchantments, and to-day I feel Victor Hugo's soul almost alien from mine. I dare not read again the books that delighted me and captured my tears at the age of fifteen. When I try to be sincere, to express only what I have really felt, I am frightened at seeing how little my impressions of the greatest writers accord with traditional judgments, and I hesitate to tell all my thought.

As a matter of fact, that tradition is almost entirely conventional and artificial. One remembers perhaps what one has felt, or rather what venerable masters have said one ought to have felt. It is, moreover, only by this docility and this understanding that a body of literary judgments can be formed and can exist. Certain minds have strength and assurance enough to establish these long series of judgments, to base them on immutable principles. Those minds, either through determination or by nature, are mirrors which change less, or, if you will, are less inventive, than the others, and the same works are always reflected in them in almost the same manner. But one easily sees that their doctrines can claim no universal assent, and that, at bottom, they are only immobilized personal preferences.

We think that what we like is good, and that is all (I am not here speaking of those who think they like what they are told is good) ; only some people always like the same things, and regard them as pleasant for all men ; others, of a less robust turn, have more variable affections, and get reconciled to this. But, dogmatic or not, and whatever its pretensions, criticism does no more than define the impression made upon us at a given moment by a given work of art in which the writer has himself noted the impression which he received from the world at some particular time.

3

Since this is the case, and since, moreover, all is vanity, let us like the books that please us without bothering ourselves about classifications and doctrines, coming to an understanding with ourselves that our impression of to-day shall not bind that of to-morrow. If such and such an acknowledged masterpiece is offensive to me, grates on me, or, what is worse, says nothing to me ; if, on the contrary, such and such a book of to-day or yesterday, though not perhaps an immortal work, moves me to the heart, gives me the impression that it completely expresses me and reveals me to myself as more intelligent than I thought I was, shall I therefore believe myself wrong and be distressed by this ? Men of genius are never entirely conscious of themselves and of their work ; almost always they have a strain of childlikeness, ignorance, absurdity ; they have a certain easiness, a crude spontaneity ; they do not know all that they do, and they do not do it quite on purpose. Above all, in these times of reflection and increasing self-consciousness, there are, besides men of genius, artists who would not exist without them, who make use of them and profit by

4

them, but who, though much less powerful, are on the whole more intelligent than those divine monsters, have a more complete knowledge and sagacity, a more refined conception of art and life. When I meet a book written by one of these men, what a joy it is ! I feel that his work is full of all that had preceded it ; I discover in it, together with the features which form his own character and his own particular temperament, the latest state of mind, the most recent state of conscience which humanity has reached. Although he is my superior, he is like me, and I am at once on an equal footing with him. I am capable, it seems to me, at some time or other of experiencing everything which he expresses.

Writers such as M. Paul Bourget or M. Anatole France give me this pleasure ; and it is whilst again reading *Le Crime de Sylvestre Bonnard* and *Le Livre de mon Ami* that these reflections came to me. I give them for what they are worth, for in a sense they are true, though I feel keenly how much truth they omit.

I

I do not speak of the power of invention which a caprice of nature has evidently granted with more liberality to some writers of our time. I say only that M. Anatole France's mind is one of the richest ' resultants ' of all the intellectual labour of this age, and that the most recent curiosities and the rarest sentiments of a period of science and restless sympathy have entered into the composition of his literary talent. How that intelligence has been formed and successively enriched, his books themselves teach us.

He was born, I believe, in an old house in the Rue de Seine or the Quai Malaquais, in the district of the second-hand booksellers and the dealers in prints and bric-à-brac. A precocious, nervous, delicate, and affectionate child, ' already surprised at living and beholding life,' he early loved pictures and books before he had opened them ; he early knew how to look at objects, to see and enjoy their colours and their forms ; knew how to appreciate old things and to interest himself in the past. The little boy was already a true child of this age of history and erudition.

One gathers from the *Désirs de Jean Servien* and *Le Livre de mon Ami* that the father of this little boy was either a bookbinder or a doctor, a candid, serious man of meditative character ; his mother was gentle, delicate, and adorably tender.   And the child will afterwards feel this double influence.

Then, like Jean Servien, he had an excellent education of the old-fashioned sort.   He trembled with artless admiration as he construed Homer and the Greek tragedians, he lived the life of the ancients, he felt the antique beauty, he knew the magic of words, he loved phrases for their harmony of linked sounds and the images which they evoked in his mind.

And it was in an ecclesiastical school that he passed his childhood, a fact which was, I think, of great advantage to him, for the exercises of piety often make the soul gentler and more tender ; purity has a better chance of being preserved in such surroundings, at least for a time, and (except in the case of some madman and some evil hearts) afterwards when faith leaves you, you remain capable of understanding it and loving it in others, you are more fair-minded and more intelligent.

7

Then, like Jean Servien, and like many writers and artists in our democratic society where talent so often rises from below, he had a poor, hard youth, with absurd loves, unbounded desires, wild aspirations for a brilliant and noble life, deceptions, sorrows. He suffered evils, by turns real and imaginary, and, as happens to well-poised tempers, he passed out of this long crisis gentler and more indulgent to men and to life ; he brought from it a virtue which, upon the whole, has notably increased in this age—pity.

Then he entered into the Parnassian group, and his mind made new acquisitions. He learnt a more whole-hearted worship of plastic beauty. He was better able to see forms and to enjoy them. He endeavoured, with other young men, to push farther than had hitherto been done the art of combining in exact form those fine words which evoke fine images. At the same time he became impregnated with the most recent philosophies. His first verses bespoke Lucretius in a new guise, Darwin, and Leconte de Lisle.

And he was also one of the most fervent of the neo-Greeks. This enthusiastic love of

Greek life, beauty, and religion has been one of the most remarkable sentiments of the last poetic generation. With it there was mingled in M. Anatole France an interest in the most singular of historical events, that which, more than anything else, has occupied some of the greatest minds of the age for the past thirty years. Whilst M. Renan was producing his delightful *Histoire des Origines du Christianisme*, M. Anatole France was writing the *Noces Corinthiennes*.

He had to write that book, for the coming of Christianity forms, for Western peoples, the heart of the great human drama. I have said elsewhere why it is that certain minds regard that event as an immense calamity, and that they seem to me to be very sure of their ground, and that a rich and completely human soul ought to be at once both Pagan and Christian. I find this soul in that fine poem the *Noces Corinthiennes*, a masterpiece too little known. I find in it a keen understanding of history, an abundant sympathy, and a form worthy of André Chénier ; and I doubt whether any one has better expressed the childish security of those souls who are charmed with the life of this world and feel themselves at home in a deified system of nature, or, on the other hand, the mystic uneasiness from whence the new religion took its birth.

That drama indeed must have troubled innumerable families during the first three centuries. The worthy Hermas, a vine-dresser of Corinth, has remained a Pagan ; his wife, Kallista, and his daughter, Daphne, are Christians. And it is, in truth, through women that the new faith was most often to penetrate into homes. Daphne is betrothed to Hippias, who is not a Christian. Kallista falls ill, and makes a vow that if God restores her to health she will consecrate her daughter's virginity to Him, not out of selfishness, but because the old woman's life is still useful to her family, to the poor, and to the faithful. Daphne sorrowfully submits. But when Hippias returns, she can no longer resist her love ; they will both flee, or rather they will go and throw themselves at Kallista's feet and soften her. Kallista arrives unexpectedly, and drives away the young man with imprecations ; but Daphne joins him at night at the ancestral tomb, and dies in his arms, for she has taken poison, and the bishop Theognis comes too late to loose her from her mother's vow.

The action, which I greatly abridge, is simple, grand, and poignant, and the principal states of mind which must have been engendered by the clash of the two religions are all represented in it. Daphne, a Christian from docility, but with imagination and heart still full of the ancient divinities, mingling with candour the worship of Christ, God of the dead, with the remembrance of the gods of life, is a charmingly delicate and truthful figure. After her mother's cruel vow, she throws the betrothal ring into the fountain of the Nymphs :

> ' O fontaine où l'on dit que dans les anciens jours
> Les nymphes ont goûté d'ineffables amours,
> Fontaine à mon enfance auguste et familière,
> Reçois de la chrétienne une offrande dernière.
> O source ! qu'à jamais ton sein stérile et froid
> Conserve cet anneau détaché de mon doigt.
> L'anneau que je reçus dans un autre espérance. . . .
> Réjouis-toi, Dieu triste à qui plaît la souffrance ! '[1]

---

[1] ' O fountain by which it is said that the nymphs enjoyed ineffable loves in the olden days, fountain august and familiar to my childhood, receive from the Christian a final offering. O spring ! let thy cold and sterile bosom preserve for ever this ring taken from my finger. The ring which I received with a far different hope. . . . Rejoice, gloomy God whom suffering pleases.'

II

When her lover returns, all nature rises within her in·an irresistible and chaste revolt ; and yet she still feels the mysterious attraction of the God ' who does not like nuptial feasts ' :

' Christ Jésus doit un jour ressusciter les siens !
Voilà ce que du moins enseignent les anciens.
Homme, tu peux tenter d'éclaircir ce mystère ;
Moi, femme, je dois croire, adorer, et me taire.
Christ est le Dieu des morts : que son nom soit béni !
Hélas ! la vie est brève et l'amour infini.' [1]

But M. Anatole France has especially loved the fair sinners of the second century of the Roman Empire, those who, exhausted by pleasures, were asking the East to give them strange gods to love, and caressing and tragic forms of worship :

' Les femmes ont senti passer dans leurs poitrines
Le mol embrasement d'un souffle oriental.
Une sainte épouvante a gonflé leurs narines
Sous des dieux apparus loin de leur ciel natal. . . .
Elle les voit si beaux ! Son ame avide et tendre,
Que le siècle brutal fatigua sans retour,

---

[1] ' Christ Jesus is some day to restore His own to life ! That, at least, is what the elders teach us. Man, thou canst attempt to solve this mystery ; I, a woman, must believe, worship, and keep silent. Christ is the God of the dead : blessed be His name ! Alas ! life is short and love is infinite.'

Cherche entre ces esprits indulgents à qui tendre
L'ardente et lourde fleur de son dernier amour. . . .
Et Leuconoé goute éperdument les charmes
D'adorer un enfant et de pleurer un dieu.' [1]

And we also, we love these women, and
because it consoled them and still consoles
spirits in pain, the religion of Jesus continues
to inspire an incurable tenderness in many who
no longer believe. We feel in the Gospel a
certain deep, mystic, and vaguely sensual
charm. We love it for the story of the Samari-
tan woman, of Mary Magdalene, and of the
woman taken in adultery. We almost imagine
to ourselves that it is the first book in which
there was goodness, pity, sympathy for the
misguided and the unrestrained, the feeling of
universal misery, almost that of the irresponsi-
bility of the miserable. And perhaps also
we enjoy the pleasure of understanding this

[1] ' Women have felt the pleasant warmth of an Oriental influence entering their bosoms. They have been inspired by a sacred fear whilst in the presence of gods who
have appeared far from their native heaven. . . . She sees
them so fair ! Her eager and tender soul, for ever wearied
by this brutal time of ours, seeks among these indulgent
spirits for one to whom to offer the ardent and heavy
flower of her last love. . . . And Leuconoe, distraught,
tastes the charms of adoring a child and weeping for a
god.'

singular book in a heterodox fashion. Finally, we love the religion of our mothers because it is perfectly mysterious, and at certain moments we are weary of knowledge which is clear but so limited, and we detach ourselves a little from it when we see how fully it satisfies commonplace minds. Like Leuconoe with her ineffable disquiet, the modern soul ' consults all the gods,' no longer in order to believe in them like the courtesan of old, but in order to understand and reverence the dreams with which the riddle of the world has inspired our ancestors, and the illusions which saved them from so much suffering. Curiosity about religions is in this age one of the most conspicuous and best of our feelings ; M. Anatole France could not fail to experience it.

In order that none of the studies which characterize our age should escape him, he wrote an exquisite dialogue on Perrault's *Fairy Tales*, in which he shows us how those stories that amuse our children have come from the solar myths invented by men in times long past. And, as was to be expected, he also wrote some literary criticism remarkable for its freedom and penetration ; and his mind expanded still more at the sight of the great variety of other minds.

At the same time he discovered, in the company of those mad and disordered persons, those visionaries whom one meets in Paris above all places, how strange man can be, and what unexpected combinations nature, aided by civilization, can realize in a human soul and countenance. He associated with the careless and whimsical Bohemians of the Chat Maigre, and he perceived how amusing the world is for him who knows the way to look at it. He noted the gestures, the tricks of manner, the fixed ideas of these queer creatures. And, by a return on himself, when he saw them in operation, he became more and more modest and indulgent. For what are the strongest and the wisest except actors who have a little better acquaintance with themselves, but who are also moved by inexorable forces, and who will never see all the wires that pull them. He had the impression that life is indeed a dream, and that if God fashions every-body's dream, and if He knows it, He must amuse Himself prodigiously.

There is another attitude, another way of

taking life, which is characteristic of this age—a sort of Stoic pessimism, an affectation of regarding all the harshness and all the absurdity of the real world and all that is inhuman in its laws, and of opposing to them an ironical resignation. It is to have in one's mind the ruthlessness of a medical student, together with a virile gentleness, without illusions, in the conduct of one's life—the particular character which moral distinction takes on in a doctor or a chemist. This attitude can, moreover, conceal a great depth of tenderness and violent passion, and this is precisely the case of René Longuemare in *Jocaste*. But René Longuemare will grow calmer as he grows older. All those endeavours, those experiments, those successive emotions, the malady of desire, neo-Hellenism, love of form, curiosity, dilettantism, almost cheerful pessimism, end in the supreme sagacity of M. Sylvestre Bonnard, Member of the Institute.

Sylvestre Bonnard is the glory of M. Anatole France. He is the most original figure that he has portrayed. He is M. Anatole France himself as he would like to be, as he will be, perhaps as he already is. Grown old ? Not at all, for, in the first place, if M. Bonnard's intellect is seventy years of age, his heart has remained young, he is able to love. And then he belongs to an age in which people become old very early. Sylvestre Bonnard sums up in himself all that is best in the soul of that age. Other ages have incarnated the best of themselves in the citizen, in the artist, in the knight, in the priest, in the man of the world : the nineteenth century in its decline, if we wish to retain only the most eminent of its qualities, is an elderly scholar, a bachelor, very intelligent, very meditative, very ironical, and very gentle.

And M. Anatole France has been able to show us this almost symbolical figure in a very living and very special manner. M. Bonnard is indeed an old bachelor, and he has many of an old bachelor's crotchets. He is tyrannized over by his old housekeeper whom he respects and whom he fears. He has a big nose whose movements betray his emotions. He has an innocent weakness for good wine and for wholesome, well-cooked food. There is in his manner of speech a touch of pedantry at which he himself is the first to smile. He gives way to a garrulity that is full of matter like one of Homer's old men who has had three thousand years of additional experience. And the memory of Homer comes in all the more pat, as, in a most delicious blend, M. Anatole France, who has been nurtured in Greek literature, takes a delight in imitating the elegance of ancient speech in order to express the most modern sentiments, and M. Bonnard's style sometimes recalls the *Odyssey* and sometimes the *Œconomicus* or the *Œdipus at Colonus*. They are indeed the discourses of a Nestor who, instead of three poor little generations, had seen a hundred and twenty elapse.

II

Now, what sort of novels would M. Sylvestre Bonnard write ? Precisely those of M. Anatole France. The habit of meditation and of retiring within oneself scarcely develops the gift of inventing stories and extraordinary combinations of events. This gift seems of even small value to aged meditative persons (at least unless it reaches as exceptional a degree as in the elder Dumas, for example). M.

Sylvestre Bonnard therefore could not write romances of adventure or even romantic novels. Add to this a fear of what is rhetorical, of the emphasis of expression which tragic stories almost always require. And, finally, what interests M. Bonnard most are not the surprises of fortune nor dramatically violent situations, but the habitual conduct of the world and of men. To the man who reflects much, everything seems singular enough, and to him who knows how to look at it the most ordinary reality is a spectacle of continual surprise.

Thus M. France-Bonnard will tell us very simple stories. A poor lad who loves an actress, and who, after some years of harassed life, is killed by chance during the Commune —that is *Jean Servien*. A good lad from Hayti who, under the strange direction of a mulatto teacher, has several times failed in his examination for the degree of Bachelor of Arts ; who, living with a band of madmen, is not even astonished, so thoughtless is he ; who, having noticed a girl in the opposite house, perceives that he loves her on the day that she leaves Paris, rushes headlong in her pursuit, and marries her on the last page—that is *Le Chat Maigre*. An old scholar sends wood one winter to his neighbour, a poor woman in childbed. The woman, become a Russian princess, rewards the old scholar's kindness by offering him a precious book which he coveted—that is *La Bûche*. Our old scholar interests himself in an orphan girl whose mother he has loved, carries her off from her boarding-school where she is unhappy, and marries her to a pupil in the Training School for the Record Office—that is *Le Crime de Sylvestre Bonnard*. These simple themes are calculated to enchant those unhappy spirits who do not care for complicated romances.

If, as a rule, the subject is trifling, the characters are alive. What characters? What human masks will an old scholar like Sylvestre Bonnard prefer to represent? Those from which he differs most must for that very reason make most impression upon him. He is as much of a thinking being as it is possible to be ; he will therefore especially depict unthinking beings, those who abandon themselves without distrust to excesses of speech and gesture, who are least in the secret of

the human comedy, eternal dupes of themselves and of the external world.   The series
of these is admirable.   There is M. Godet-
Laterrasse, the mulatto thinker, so worthy,
so full of that enormous and jovial vanity
which one finds in negroes and half-negroes
and in some Southerners from the extreme
South.   There is the ineffable Telemachus,
formerly a negro General, who has now become
a dealer in wine, and who falls into amusing
ecstasies before the cast-off garments of his
past glory.   And among our own kind there
are all those who remind us most of the
thoughtlessness and vanity of these worthy
negroes—grave and grotesque Bohemians,
sublime failures, those who are a quarter of
a man of genius, imaginative persons, and
maniacs.   These unthinking creatures will
always have a great attraction for men devoted
to the inner life.   Here is the Marquis Tudesco,
the Italian exile, the old emphatic and learned
buffoon, who has translated Tasso, and who
solemnly gets drunk in the extravagant
uniform of an ' inspector of tunnels ' of the
Commune.   Here is M. Fellaire de Sizac, a
business man whom one would say had escaped

out of Alphonse Daudet's gallery. Here is M. Haviland, a taciturn Englishman who collects in bottles waters from all the rivers of the world. Here is Branchut the philosopher, Dion the poet, Labanne the sculptor, and how many others !

And Sylvestre Bonnard should also love creatures who are gentle, good, virtuous, or heroic, without knowing it, or rather without trying and because that is their nature— Madame de Cabry, the adorable Jeanne Alexandre, the little Madame Coccoz, afterwards Princess Trépof, even Uncle Victor, although his heroism is mixed with abominable faults, and Thérese, the sulky and faithful servant, abounding in proverbial expressions, rich in prejudices, in virtue, and in devotion.

But although he knows how to describe these figures with one salient stroke, he always observes them from the point of view of a philosopher who has acquired the faculty of being astonished that the world is what it is. He sees them not entirely in themselves, but as forming part of that stupefying whole which is the world, and testifying to what an extent the world is unintelligible. He paints them exact and living, but reverberated, if I may say so, in the mind of an old sage who knows much and has dreamed a great deal.

III

Thus he ought to end by writing novels in which he himself will be on the stage, and which will be his own history as much as that of others—corners of reality illustrated and commented on by his own ingenious experience. And such in fact are those two masterpieces, *La Bûche* and *Le Crime de Sylvestre Bonnard*. When one knows so much and reflects so much, one no longer forgets oneself, one no longer ever goes outside oneself—it is always oneself that one beholds, since one involuntarily attaches all that one observes to a general conception of the world, and this conception is in ourselves.

From this it must not be thought that those two little romances are of the same family as those of Xavier de Maistre, or, to mention a lesser artist, of M. Alphonse Karr ; to those ' humorist ' romances of which Flaubert has said in *Bouvard et Pécuchet*, that 'the author interrupts himself every moment in order to talk about his mistress and his slippers. Such a free-and-easy manner at first delighted them and then seemed to them stupid.' In the first place, it is not the author but M. Sylvestre Bonnard who speaks, and we have seen that he has his own manner and his own physiognomy. And M. Sylvestre Bonnard is far too serious to converse with us 'about his slippers or his mistress.' If he speaks of his cat, it is because his cat is for him a natural and necessary companion who has his place in his study, and in order to address to him speeches full of juice and philosophy. If perhaps these little stories, owing to some of the reflections with which they are interspersed, make us think of Sterne's *Sentimental Journey*, at least they are composed with care and the digressions are only apparent. They are continuous stories which have been enriched by passing through a very alert mind, furnished with a great number of memories and a great deal of knowledge.

This vision of little portions of the human comedy by an old member of the Institute who

is very learned and very good, is as delicious
as one can imagine.

Its charm is very complex, and I feel that
I shall never be able to disentangle all its
elements.   First of all, there is a very gentle,
very calm irony which insinuates itself into all
the narratives and all the reflections.   The very
drawing of the characters has always something ironical ; it accentuates, with a placid
exaggeration, the characteristic features.   For
example, M. Mouche and Mademoiselle Pré-
fère, two venerable persons, serenely hypo-
critical and thoroughly ill-natured, say indeed
what they ought to say, but they do not say
it exactly as they would in reality : their
remarks, like their appearance, reach us
reverberated and reflected.   This continual
and almost involuntary irony is in truth the
habitual tone of a man who beholds his own and
other people's lives, and for whom everything
is appearance, phenomenon, spectacle ;   for
such a fashion of taking the world does not
exist without a detachment of the mind which
is necessarily ironical. One retains one's
coolness even in the most assiduous observation or in the strongest emotion, and in spite

of oneself one carries everywhere the mental reservation that all is vanity. And all the personages who do not hold this belief, even those whom you love, make you smile in some way or other, were it the most affectionately in the world.

    ' " Yes, my friend," said M. Bonnard to the little almanac-seller who offered him the *Key to Dreams* ; " but these dreams and a thousand others also, joyous or tragic, are summed up in a single one, the dream of life, and will your little almanac give me the key to that ? " '

The highest wisdom never fails to smile at itself ; M. Sylvestre Bonnard has always that smile.

But this irony, being on the whole only an ever-present consciousness of the mystery of things and of the fragility of human destinies, implies kindness, pity, tenderness—a tenderness full of thought and thus all the more profound. There are I don't know how many pages that bring tears to your eyes : those in which M. Bonnard remembers Clémentine, those in which he goes to kneel at her tomb with Madame de Gabry, those in which he confesses that he had not reckoned that Jeanne would marry so quickly. And what do you say to this little speech to Jeanne:

'Jeanne, listen to me still. You have hitherto made yourself agreeable to my housekeeper, who, like all old people, is naturally rather morose. Share her susceptibilities. I have thought that I ought to do so myself and to put up with her impatience. I shall say to you, "Jeanne: Respect her." And in speaking thus I do not forget that she is my servant and yours; she will not forget it either. But in her you ought to respect her great age and her great heart. She is an humble creature who has continued a long time in what is good; she has become hardened in it. Bear with the stiffness of that upright soul. Know how to command; she will know how to obey. Go, my child; arrange your room in the way that seems most suitable to you for your work and your repose.'

And this beautiful invocation:

'From where you are to-day, Clémen-

tine, I say to myself, behold this heart
now grown cold with age, but whose blood
formerly boiled for you, and say if it does
not revive at the thought of loving what
remains of you on earth. All passes
away, for you have passed away ; but
life is immortal ; it is she that must be
loved in her forms unceasingly re-created.
The rest is a child's game, and I with my
books am like a little child who is playing
with knuckle-bones. The end of life is
you, Clémentine, who have revealed it to
me.'

Is it my fault, finally, if I cannot read the
last pages of *Le Crime de Sylvestre Bonnard*
without a great desire to weep ?

'Poor Jeanne, poor mother !

'I am too old to remain very sensitive ;
but, in truth, the death of a child is a
saddening mystery.

'To-day the father and mother have
come back for six weeks beneath the old
man's roof. . . . Jeanne slowly mounts
the stairs, embraces me, and murmurs
in my ear some words which I divine
rather than hear. And I answer her :

"God bless you, Jeanne, you and your husband, in your most distant posterity! *Et nunc dimittis servum tuum, Domine.*"'

Everywhere this tenderness and this irony accompany one another, for they have the same origin; they are both such that they presuppose not only a natural disposition of the mind and heart, but extensive knowledge, the habit of meditation, long reveries on man and on the world, and an acquaintance with the philosophies that have attempted to explain this double mystery.

This serious basis of general ideas is never absent ; often, unexpectedly, in reference to some particular observation, it appears as if in a flash, and one suddenly sees, behind the recollection or the impression that is noted in passing, distant views which stir one and make one think, disclosing themselves by the virtue of words.

Here is an example of this, which I have chosen for its clearness. Another writer would say, I suppose, when speaking of the garden in which his childhood was passed, ' It is in this garden that I played when I was quite a child.' M. Anatole France writes : ' It is in this garden that I learnt whilst playing *to know some portions of this old universe.*'

Here is a young couple coming back from a walk :

'They are coming back arm in arm from the forest. Jeanne is wrapped in a black shawl, and Henri wears crape on his straw hat ; but they are both glowing with youth, and they smile gently at one another. They smile on the earth that bears them, on the air that bathes them, on the light that each sees shining in the other's eyes. I make a sign to them from my window with my handkerchief, and they smile at my old age."

Do you not feel how each little picture grows, and how the whole universe comes and mingles with it ?

'Stars *which have shone on the light or heavy head of all my forgotten ancestors*, it is through your clearness that I feel a sad regret awakening within me. I should like to have a son *who would still see you* when I shall be no more.'

Is it possible to include more contemplation

in a regret, and more thought in a simple glance at the stars?

But this knowledge which is at once irony and tenderness and which heightens all feelings and all impressions, is the knowledge of an old scholar, of a member of the Institute. Thence arise on many occasions effects that are delicately and delightfully comic owing to the unexpected contrast between certain ideas and objects and M. Sylvestre Bonnard's gravity, integrity, scientific exactness, and, at other times, the antique beauty of his language. Thus, when the good man is suddenly roused from his reflections by M. Paul de Gabry:

> 'I have reason to believe that my countenance betrayed my unseemly distraction by a certain expression of stupidity which it assumes in the majority of social transactions.'

And what do you say to this description, with its assigned reasons, of a woman's beauty:

> 'Her face and her form were those of an adult woman. The amplitude of her bodice and the roundness of her figure left no doubt in this respect even in an

old scholar like me. I shall add, without fear of being mistaken, that she was very beautiful and of a proud bearing, for my iconographical studies for a long time past have accustomed me to recognize the purity of a type and the character of a countenance.'

I could quote numerous examples of this form of comedy. The coolness, the good-nature, the slow dignity of the old archæologist registering amusing observations, resemble somewhat the *humour* of Sterne or of Dickens (add that M. Anatole France is also able to depict in the manner of Dickens or of M. Alphonse Daudet) ; but, at the same time, M. Bonnard's humour is expressed in a purer, more rhythmical, more harmonious language, in a language nurtured in Greek beauty and grace. Read again and again, and enjoy at length, I beg you, this exquisite harangue by an old scholar to an old cat :

' " Hamilcar," said I to him, as I stretched out my legs, " Hamilcar, somnolent prince of the city of books, nocturnal guardian ! Like the divine cat who fought the impious in the city of Heliopolis during the night of the great combat, thou dost defend against vile rodents the books which the old scholar acquires at the cost of moderate savings and indefatigable zeal. In this library which thy military virtues protect, Hamilcar, sleep with the indolence of a Sultana. For thou dost unite in thy person the formidable aspect of a Tartar warrior with the heavy grace of a woman of the East. Heroic and voluptuous Hamilcar, sleep waiting for the hour when the mice will dance by the light of the moon before the *Acta Sanctorum* of the learned Bollandists."'

IV

Insinuating as is the melancholy of M. Sylvestre Bonnard's private journal, do not let yourself be caught by it ; and if you are too much moved, tell yourself that it did not happen. For Clémentine did not die, M. Bonnard married, and he wrote *Le Livre de mon Ami*.

That book will please mothers, for it speaks of children. It will charm women, for it is delicate and pure. It will delight poets, for it is full of the most natural and the subtlest poetry. It will satisfy philosophers, for need I say that one continually feels in it the habit of serious meditation ? It will have the esteem of psychologists, for they will find in it the most flowing description of the movements of a childlike soul. It will satisfy old humanists, for it breathes of the love of good letters. It will captivate tender souls, for it is full of tenderness. And it will find favour with the disillusioned, for irony is not absent from it, and it reveals more of resignation than of optimism.

What ! All that in some impressions of childhood ? It is so, and there is nothing surprising about it, except the writer's talent, for there is no better subject for an observer who is a poet, nor for a poet who is a philosopher, nor for a philosopher who is a father.

In the first place, a little child, when he is pretty or even when he is not ugly, is the most agreeable creature in the world to see, the most graceful in his movements and his whole gait, the noblest in his ignorance of evil, his powerlessness to be wicked or base or unworthy. A little child is also the most loved by other beings to whom he is the reason for living, for whom he is the supreme affection, the dearest hope, often the only interest. And, above all, a little child is to a philosopher like Sylvestre Bonnard the most attractive object of observation. He is a quite new man, not deformed, perfectly original ; he is the being who receives the most direct and vivid impressions of the things of the entire world, for whom everything is astonishment and fairyland ; who, seeking to comprehend the world, imagines incomplete explanations which respect its mystery and are for that reason eminently poetical. Later on, the average man accepts explanations which he believes to be definitive; he loses the gift of being aston-ished, of marvelling, of feeling the mystery of things. Those who preserve this gift are the very few, and they are the poets and the true philosophers. Every child is a poet by nature. The soul of a well-endowed little child is nearer that of Homer than the soul of this or that citizen or mediocre Academician.

And in another respect the little child, although superior to the man, is already a

man. He already experiences his passions :
vanity, self-love, jealousy—love also—desire of
glory, aspiration to beauty. His good movements, being spontaneous, have in him a divine
grace. And as for those which spring from
egoism, being inoffensive and unpremeditated,
they are amusing to see. They only appear
as piquant manifestations of the instinct of
self-preservation and conquest, as the first
and innocent engagements in the necessary
struggle for existence.

M. Anatole France has represented, after
others, after Victor Hugo, after Madame Alphonse Daudet, some of these aspects of childhood, that progressive awakening of the life
of thought and of the life of the passions—but
in his own manner, in a more philosophical
spirit and with a more penetrating analysis.
What he relates, moreover, is the impressions
of a specially endowed little child, a child who
will be an artist, a contemplator, a dreamer,
who, above all, will regard the world as a
spectacle for the eyes and a problem for
thought, not as a field of battle or as a provision
shop in which the main business is to secure
one's own share. And the character of this

little child is defined more clearly by the neigh-
bourhood of another child endowed with
different qualities, better armed for struggle
and for action, the little Fontanet, ' as ingenious as Ulysses,' so sly, so sharp, so clever, who
will become ' a lawyer, a county councillor, a
manager of companies, a Member of Parlia-
ment.'

Is it necessary to recall some touches from
these stories of childhood ?   It is very embar-
rassing to do so ; what I shall quote will cause
me remorse for seeming to neglect what I do
not quote :

> ' Tout dans l'immortelle nature
>   Est miracle aux petits enfants.
>
>   .   .   .   .
>
>   Ils font de frissons en frisson
>   La découverte de la vie.' [1]

' I was happy.   A thousand things at
once familiar and mysterious occupied my
imagination, a thousand things that were
nothing in themselves, but that made up
part of my life.   It was very tiny, my
life ; but it was a life—that is to say, the

[1] ' Everything in immortal nature is a miracle to
little children. . . . They shudder at every step they
make in the discovery of life.'

centre of things, the middle of the world.
Do not smile at what I say, or smile at
it only in friendship and think of it :
whoever lives, were it only a little dog, is
in the middle of things.'

The paper in the little room where Pierre
Noziere plays is covered with rosebuds, small,
modest, all of them alike, all pretty :

'One day, in the little room, laying
aside her embroidery, my mother lifted
me up in her arms ; then showing me one
of the paper flowers, she said to me :

' " I give you that rose."

'And in order to recognize it, she
marked it with a cross with her bodkin.

' Never did a present make me happier.'

I recommend to you also as marvels of the
psychology of childhood the chapter about
Alphonse and the grape, and that in which
Pierre, wishing to become a hermit and to
renounce the goods of this world, throws his
toys out of the window :

' " That child is stupid," cried my
father, shutting the window.

' I felt anger and shame at hearing myself
judged thus. But I considered that my

father, not being a saint like me, would not share with me the glory of the blessed, *and this thought was a great consolation to me.'*

One of the most original merits of the book is that the child who is its hero is indeed ' in the middle of the world.' The characters who pass through its chapters—the Abbé Jubal, Father Le Beau, Mademoiselle Lefort—are indeed seen by a little child. The stories of grown-up persons not understood, incompletely seen, like series of strange scenes which are not connected with one another, assume the airs and proportions of dreams. Look at what becomes in a child's brain of the story of the lady in white whose husband is travelling and who is loved by another gentleman. Look, above all, at how the story of the pretty foster-mother becomes fantastic, that of Marcelle with the golden eyes, the poor creature of love and madness—an apparition of a very good, very capricious, and very unhappy fairy. And what sweetness there is in the man's pity flowing out afterwards over the child's vision !

' Poor soul in pain, poor soul wandering

on the ancient Ocean which rocked the
first loves of the earth, dear phantom, O
my foster-mother and my fairy ! be blessed
by the most faithful of your lovers, by
perhaps the only one who still remembers
you ! Be blessed for the gift that you
placed in my cradle merely by leaning
over it ; be blessed for having revealed
to me, when I was scarcely born to
thought, the delicious torments which
beauty gives to souls eager to comprehend
it ; be blessed by him who was the child
you lifted up from the ground in order
to find out the colour of his eyes ! That
child was the happiest, and I dare say the
best, of your friends. It is to him that
you gave the most, O generous woman !
for you opened to him, along with your two
arms, the infinite world of dreams.'

Alas ! perhaps this is supreme wisdom—
to see the world and to marvel at it like all
little ones, but only to return to that wonder
after having passed through all the wisdoms
and all the philosophies ; to conceive of the
world as a tissue of inexplicable phenomena,
in the manner of children, but by long, round-

about ways and for reasons that children do not know.

This is what M. Anatole France does. His contemplation is full of memories. I know no writer in whom reality is reflected through a richer medium of knowledge, of literature, of anterior impressions and meditations. M. Hugues Le Roux said in an elegant *Chinoiserie*: ' All the things of this world are reflected, the bridges of jade in the streams of the gardens, the open heavens in the surface of the rivers, love in memory. The poet, bending over this world of appearances, prefers to the moon which is rising over the mountains that which lights her lamp in the depth of the waters, and the memory of dead love to the present pleasures of love.' Well, for M. Anatole France, things have a habit of being reflected two or three times ; for besides being reflected in one another, they are also reflected in books before being reflected in his own mind. ' There is nothing in the world for me except words, so much of a philologist am I,' says Sylvestre Bonnard. ' Each of us dreams the dream of life in his own way. I dream that dream in my library.' But the dream one dreams in a

library so as to enrich it with the dream of
many other men, does not cease to be personal.
M. Anatole France's stories are, above all, the
stories of a great scholar, of an excessively
learned and subtle mandarin ; but out of all
the proffered booty he has made a choice which
was determined by his own temperament, by
his own originality ; and perhaps it would not
be a bad definition of him to say that he is a
learned and tender humorist in love with
antique beauty. It is remarkable, at any
rate, that this rich intelligence owes almost
nothing (unlike M. Paul Bourget) to the literatures of the North ; it seems to me to be the
extreme and very pure product of the Greek
and Latin tradition alone.

I perceive, as I end, that I have not said
at all what I intended to say. M. Anatole
France's books are those which I should most
like to have written. I believe I understand
and feel them completely ; but I love them so
much that I have not been able to analyse them
without a little agitation.

PAUL BOURGET

I DO not remember ever to have felt an embarrassment comparable with that which I feel in speaking of the work and literary personality of M. Paul Bourget. Its richness, its apparent complexity, bewilder me. I see him in one fashion ; but immediately afterwards I see him in another. The idea most commonly formed of him is that of an affected, subtle, feminine person, of a sort of dandy of letters, very elegant, very refined, very cajoling. But this is far from being the complete man. For, on the contrary, several of the pages he has written (perhaps the greater number) are especially remarkable for the virile vigour and fine lucidity of an essentially philosophical intelligence. And, in the same way, he can appear in many passages as a pure dilettante, a dilettante of the decadence, full of affectation and artifice, of an unwholesome sensuality

43

and an ambiguous mysticism ; but suddenly one discovers in him a very grave spirit, with the gravity of a priest, very much preoccupied with the moral life, serious to the point of taking everything tragically.

His style presents the same contrasts : he is affected and he is forcible ; he is pedantic and he is simple ; frozen by abstractions, stiff and stilted, and then suddenly graceful and languishing, or full, coloured, and robust. He is excellent, and he is little short of detestable. And one is astonished that the cruel opening of *Cruelle Enigme*, and the adorable account of the meeting of the lovers at Folkestone, or the powerful picture of the duel of the sexes in love, in the style of the plays of the younger Dumas, have come from the same hand. And as I turn over those latter beautiful pages, I am imperatively arrested by brilliant phrases like this, which ends a paragraph about the part played by love in the development of our moral being : ' All through our years thus there is enriched or impoverished, at the hazard of this sovereignly beneficent or destructive power, the treasure of acquired morality of which we are the depositories ; faithless depositories so often, preparing, amid caresses and smiles, the bankruptcy of our successors.' Or this passage dazzles me like a magnificent flash of lightning: 'Love alone has remained irreducible, like death, to human conventions. It is untamed and free in spite of codes and fashions. The woman who undresses in order to give herself to a man, rids herself with her clothing of her whole social personality ; she becomes again for him whom she loves what he becomes again for her, a natural and solitary creature whose happiness is guaranteed by no protection, whose unhappiness can be removed by no decree.' I am delighted with this beauty of thought and form ; but I turn over the page and I find a ' flowering time ' or an ' abortion ' which ' is derived' from a certain quality of love. I find there that ' the Lady ' is a superior and charming being, ' *made of unshaken security,*' as if the security was in the lady and not in the adorer. Or there are gasping mannerisms of language : ' What to do against that ? To kneel before the dolorous sister and adore her for being dolorous.'

These things grieve me, and my embarrassment redoubles. . . . The most penetrat-

45

ing and most vigorous intelligence, and with it
a morbid debility, pedantry also, and certain
intellectual predilections that resemble superstition, and a taste for certain elegances which
one might almost take for snobbishness—how
is one to see clearly in all this ?

II

Add that M. Paul Bourget is doubtless a
poet and a novelist, but is perhaps above all a
critic—and not a critic who judges and relates,
but a critic who understands and feels, who has
especially striven to picture to himself different
states of soul, to make them his own. Among
so many souls which he penetrates and assimilates, where is his own ?

It seems at first sight that the more a critic
had breadth of mind and power of sympathy,
the fewer individual traits he would present
to the writer who desired to define and to paint
him. The most marked, the most original,
not only among men, but among writers, are
those who do not understand at all, who do
not feel at all, who do not love at all, whose
knowledge, intelligence, and tastes are clearly

46

bounded. The ideal man who will come at the end of time, as·he will know and conceive equally of all things, will doubtless have hardly any intellectual personality ; and he will only have very attenuated passions, vices, and eccentricities. The members of the small philosophical oligarchy who, according to M. Renan, will perhaps one day govern the world, delivered by omniscience from inferior passions, should resemble one another to such a degree that they will be almost indistinguishable from each other. They will approximate to God, the great scholar and the great critic ; and God has no individuality. This very day the critic who would form an entire and thorough notion of all the aspects under which the world has been reflected in men's minds, could hardly be defined except by that very aptitude for penetrating and embracing everything.

We have not yet reached that point. In reality there are as many ways of understanding criticism as there are of understanding fiction, drama or poetry ; the personality of the writer —when he has one—can therefore be equally strongly impressed upon his criticism. Only a little more care is sometimes needed in order to detach it..

It is too evident (I have need of these truisms in order that I may recover confidence) that, like any other writer, a critic necessarily puts into his writings his own temperament and his own conception of life, since it is with his own mind that he describes other minds ; that the differences are as profound between M. Taine, M. Nisard, and Sainte-Beuve, as between—let us say, between Corneille, Racine, and Molière , and, finally, that criticism is a representation of the world as personal, as relative, as vain, and consequently as interesting, as those which constitute the other literary forms.

Criticism varies infinitely according to the object studied, according to the mind which studies it, according to the point of view in which that mind places itself. It can consider works, men, or ideas. And it can judge or merely define. At first dogmatic, it has become historical and scientific ; but to all appearance its evolution has not ended. Vain as a doctrine, necessarily incomplete as a science, it tends perhaps to become simply the art of enjoying books, and of enriching and refining its impressions by means of them.

M. Nisard begins by forming a general and, as it were, purified idea of the French genius. He has deduced this idea from a first glance at the whole of our literature. He makes the beliefs of spiritual philosophy enter into it as an integral part. With the ideal thus conceived, he compares the works of writers, and extols or maltreats them as they approach it more or less closely. For the rest, he isolates those works, most often neglects the persons of their writers ; or, if he speaks of them, it is in order to attribute to them, in the name of free-will, the merit or the dishonour of having served or betrayed the ideal which he has defined at the beginning. He does not grasp any necessary bond between the works and their producers, between the latter and their social environment, or between successive epochs. And yet his *History* unrolls according to an inexorable plan, and the French spirit in his writings resembles a moral personality who develops and then declines throughout the ages. Hence his *History* possesses a rigorous unity. It is very systematic and singularly

49

partial and incomplete ; but how interesting is M. Nisard's mind ! how subtle, delicate, and contemptuous it is !

M. Taine, in his *History of English Literature*, does the direct contrary and yet does the same thing. Whilst M. Nisard only considered the actual books, M. Taine affects especially to consider the near or distant causes of which they are the result ; and whilst M. Nisard cuts off the books from their roots, M. Taine studies those roots down to their utmost ramifications and the very soil in which they are buried. But this explanation of the books by the men, and of the men by the race and the environment, is often only a snare. For the critic has first of all formed, without saying so, by a first rapid review of English literature, an idea of the English genius (as M. Nisard did of the genius of France), and it is from this that he deduces the conditions and the environment in which works that are specifically English could be produced. And then, all those which this environment does not explain, he affects to lay aside. He thus reaches by another road an exclusiveness as narrow as that of M. Nisard. The spiritualism of the one, the positivism of

the other, end therefore in an analogous result.
And we can say, as we said just now : M.
Taine's *History* is singularly systematic, partial, and incomplete ; but how interesting is
M. Taine's genius ! What a power of generali-
zation, and, at the same time, what magic of
colour in the work of this poet-logician !

Thus, whether dogmatic or scientific, literary
criticism is never, in the end, more than the
personal and decrepit work of a miserable
human being. Sainte-Beuve blends the two
methods with much grace, sometimes appreci-
ates, but more often describes, still judges
works in accordance with tradition and in the
classic taste, but enlarges that tradition, applies
himself more readily, by wandering over the
whole field of literature, to the construction of
moral portraits and biographies, and furnishes
I don't know how many scattered but exquisite
fragments towards what he called the natural
history of men's minds.

I pass over the various combinations of
doctrine, history, and psychology proper to
MM. Scherer, Montégut, and Brunetière. But
either I am greatly mistaken or M. Paul
Bourget has imagined an almost new form of

criticism. Criticism becomes for M. Bourget the history of his own intellectual and moral formation. It is, so to say, *egotist* criticism. His mind being eminently and almost uniquely a product of this century's end (the influence of the Græco-Latin tradition is little marked in his case), he confines himself to the writers of the last thirty years, and chooses from among them those with whom he finds himself in conformity of head and heart. And he does not paint their portraits or write their biographies : he does not analyse their works and study their methods of procedure ; he does not define the impression that their books have made upon him considered as works of art. He only seeks to explain and describe such of their states of conscience and such of their ideas as he has best appropriated by imitation and sympathy. And thus, whilst at bottom only writing the history of his own soul, at the same time he writes the history of the most original sentiments of his generation, and thus constructs a considerable—and definitive— fragment of the moral history of our epoch.

III

One means of knowing M. Paul Bourget
would be to do for him what he has done for
the ten writers who figure in his *Essais de
Psychologie Contemporaine*. It would be a
question of seeking, to use his own expression,
' what ways of feeling and tasting life he
proposes to those who are younger than he is '
—or to those of his own generation. For it
seems that M. Paul Bourget has a rather great
influence on the young people of the present
day, not perhaps on those who have carried classical studies to some length, and
who are fortified and defended by the Latin
and Gallic tradition, but on the more restless, the more nervous, the more ignorant
section of the young people who write. In vain
has the Academy honoured him publicly ; this
does not prevent the more adventurous among
the younger school of writers and those with
the most troubled brains, the symbolists,
æsthetes, Wagnerians, and Mallarmists, from
being full of respect for him, from regarding
him as a master. And, besides, he has all
the young women on his side. Perhaps no one,
at the present moment, inspires a more tender

53

devotion in certain souls. He is, for many, the pre-eminent poet, the friend, the consoler, almost the spiritual director. On the other hand, many ripe men, especially among old-fashioned folk and among those who are deeply impregnated with classical letters, cannot endure him. But, whether one likes him or not, it must be admitted that his mind is one of the richest and most distinguished results of the literary and moral culture of the second half of the century.

What is first of all eminent in him is precisely this intellectual and sentimental curiosity, this aptitude and also this effort to know, to experience, and to understand the most recent states of soul as they manifest themselves in the books of our most original writers. He himself thus sums up the precious contents of his *Essais* :

'In reference to M. Renan and the Goncourt brothers, I have indicated the germ of melancholy that is enveloped in dilettantism. I have attempted to show, in reference to Stendhal, Tourgeniev, and Amiel, some of the fatal consequences of cosmopolitan life. The poems of Baudel aire and the comedies of M. Dumas have furnished me with a pretext for analysing several fine shades of modern love and for indicating the perversions or the incapacities of that love under the pressure of the spirit of analysis. Gustave Flaubert and MM. Leconte de Lisle and Taine have permitted me to show some examples of the effects produced by science on various imaginations and sensibilities. I have been able, in reference also to M. Renan, the Goncourts, M. Taine, and Flaubert, to study several cases of conflict between democracy and the higher culture.'

There, in fact, is the complete inventory of the sentiments, the anxieties, and the torments imagined and experienced by the modern soul.

M. Bourget prides himself on comprehending this soul, of loving it in its entirety, even in its most morbid and most ephemeral manifestations. He has strange partialities for the obscure and mystic poetry of the latest little coteries (and this has gained him their veneration). He will not have it said that any mental predilection of his time has been alien from him or has not been understood by him. This is a rare critical scruple. Similarly, as cosmopolitanism appears to him to be one of the signs of our age, he has been a cosmopolitan, he has set himself to be one. He has lived in London and in Florence as much as in Paris. He has even stayed in Spain and Morocco, and, I ask you, what could Morocco say to him, to him the meditative man, the man of inner dreams? Similarly also, he affects to know and love the latest refinements of contemporary luxury; he would be angry with himself for having been ignorant of a single detail of the most elegant manner of living invented by the latest products of civilization. This belongs to him, this is his province in the same manner as is dilettantism or cosmopolitanism. And this is why this psychologist, who is but rarely and feebly a landscape artist, is often enough an upholsterer.

However, among the sentiments which M. Paul Bourget defines and explains with a like precision, we distinguish those which he experiences naturally and which he prefers, and those which he makes some effort to appropriate, and we can discover, among the writers that engage his attention, which are they whom he most esteems.

From Baudelaire, for whom his predilection is very marked, he seems to have taken a singular mixture of sensuality and mysticism, a sort of rather depraved Catholicism. This sentiment is very peculiar to our age. It is a hundred miles away from the classical eroticism. It presupposes a somewhat debilitated race, a diminution of muscular force and a refinement of the nervous system, the persistence of the spirit of analysis even in the midst of sensations best calculated to make you lose your head, and consequently a certain incapacity for the full and tranquil enjoyment of the pleasures of the body, the feeling of this incapacity, a paradoxical return, at the height of debauch, to contempt for the flesh, and even in pollution, a half-feigned and half-sincere aspiration towards purity which sharpens the savour of the sin and transforms it into an intellectual sin, into a sin of malice.

From M. Renan he takes aristocratic dis-

dain and especially dilettantism, ' that disposition of mind, at once very intelligent and
very voluptuous, which in turn inclines us
towards the various forms of life, and leads
us to lend ourselves to all those forms without giving ourselves to any of them ' ; from
M. Taine he takes the scientific temper, certain habits of composition and of language,
and a fondness for large generalizations ;
from M. Dumas the younger (an unexpected
thing) he takes a tragic preoccupation with
the moral questions in the dramas of love.

From Flaubert, the Goncourts, M. Leconte
de Lisle, and, in general, from all the purely
' artistic ' writers (however modern, moreover, may be their basis of latent philosophy)
it does not seem that M. Paul Bourget takes
much, although he understands them marvellously.

But Stendhal has his whole affection.
Stendhal is his passion, his vice, and sometimes his prejudice. Stendhal is the only
writer anterior to the generation of 1850 whom
he has admitted into his gallery. He always
utters his name with a little mystery, like
that of the god of a secret religion. ' Henri

Beyle,' the name takes on for him the sweetness of a pet name—or the importance of a sacred and hidden name that is revealed only to adepts. He says ' Henri Beyle ' as a devotee of Molière says ' Poquelin.' This cult is here very legitimate, Stendhal having employed, with more sureness, subtlety, boldness, and connection than any other writer, the instrument which M. Bourget has himself used to probe the most characteristic sentiments of his generation or to make them live in himself—analysis.

Thus we are led to notice two other characteristics of M. Paul Bourget's mind. This inquisitive person is an analyst and a pessimist (a ' melancholiac ' if you prefer it). Let us not separate the two things, for in him they are closely bound together. M. Bourget is very clearly one of those who are less preoccupied with the external world than with the world of the soul ; less sensitive to the pleasure of seeing and rendering the forms of things or the various aspects of the human scramble than to that of decomposing sentiments and ideas into their primitive elements and of tracing one moral phenomenon to another until he finds one that is irreducible. Now, the spirit of analysis ends naturally in a great sadness. Why? Because this last irreducible element is always a fatal instinct or an unsatisfied desire. What M. Bourget ends by reaching in the depth of the souls that he studies is always (whatever be the form it assumes and with whatever shades it may embellish itself on the surface) the feeling of the necessity of things—or of the disproportion between the ideal and the real, between our dream and our destiny. And that is sad.

There are, if I may so express myself, two degrees of this sadness. M. Paul Bourget tells us that all the sentimental states which he has analysed lead to pessimism. It is the spectre of pessimism which he sees standing at the end of all the paths he has traced out in what Shakespeare calls the forest of souls. For Baudelairism, even in its accommodations with the flesh, implies the consciousness of its indignity, and a vision of universal sin. Dilettantism, that gift of imagining the most diverse moral lives with precision and sympathy, implies the impossi-

bility of resting in any of them. Intellectual
aristocracy has to pay for its existence by a
painful sensitiveness in regard to all the vul-
garities of real life. Cosmopolitanism, which
shows you the immensity and the variety of
the world, almost at the same moment makes
you feel its monotony and its uselessness ; the
planet appears smaller to him who knows it
better. Look at the state to which exoticism,
which is the picturesque form of cosmopolitanism, has led Pierre Loti. The scientific
spirit condemns you to the spectacle of a
world governed by blind forces and which
lacks goodness. And so on.—And if those
various forms of seeing and feeling are very
melancholy in themselves, the analysis of each
of them doubles their sadness by showing
us that they are incurable.—In brief, to know
is to be sad, because all knowledge ends in
the recognition of the unknowable and in
that of the vanity of human beings. Judge,
then, if M. Bourget can be light-hearted,
not having to console himself the violent
distractions, the life of action, and the robust
temperament of his master, Stendhal.

M. Bourget has, however, denied that he is

a pessimist. He is wrong ! A pessimist is not necessarily a man who affirms the predominance of evil over good in the universe, nor a misanthrope, nor a hypochondriac, nor a man who has given up hope. Every man who reflects on human destiny and finds it unintelligible, and has neither Christian faith nor simple-minded belief in progress to comfort him, can be called a pessimist. The bare fact of understanding nothing in the world and of seeing no explanation of it is, when one thinks of it, sad enough. This does not prevent one from living like other people, from enjoying, when the chance offers, the sunshine, pure air, or even the society of men and women ; but, during the moments when one thinks, it is hardly possible, without a positive faith, to be an optimist : there are too many absurd and useless sufferings, and, on all sides, too thick a wall of night. . . . M. Bourget denies in vain. His very style has a tone which one does not mistake ; it gives forth a plaintive, lamenting, weeping sound. . . .

Doubtless the absence of positive belief and the spirit of analysis can turn into heedlessness in some people (look at Montaigne), but

not in those whose sensibility to moral good
and evil is exceptionally developed. Now,
M. Paul Bourget has one of these latter consciences. And that, I believe, is his last and
most intimate characteristic. He himself defines and distinguishes between the moralist
and the psychologist somewhere or other
with much force :

    ' The moralist,' he says, ' is very close
to the psychologist in the object of his
study, for both are curious to reach the
secret depths of the soul and desire to
know the springs of men's actions. But
to the psychologist this curiosity suffices.
This knowledge has its end in itself. . . .
He sees the birth of ideas, their development, their combination, impressions of
the senses resulting in emotions and in
reasonings, states of conscience always
in process of being made and unmade, a
complex and changing vegetation of the
mind and of the heart. Vainly does the
moralist declare some of these states of
conscience criminal, some of those com-
plications contemptible, some of those
changes hateful. The psychologist hardly

63

understands what is meant by crime or contempt or indignation . . . He even delights in the description of dangerous states of soul which revolt the moralist ; he takes pleasure in understanding base actions if those actions reveal an energetic nature, and if the profound labour which they manifest appears singular to him. In a word, the psychologist analyses solely in order to analyse, and the moralist analyses so as to judge.'

Well, then, whatever be the abyss M. Bourget pleases to dig between these two species of minds, if one cannot say that he himself is truly a moralist, he is not a pure psychologist either. At least he is a psychologist who is very much tormented by moral questions, very much moved, very anxious, sometimes frightened. He is habitually uneasy as to the consequences which the ideas he expounds can have on the happiness and moral well-being of humanity. He often exclaims (in more distinguished terms and without throwing up his arms, but rather with his hands over his eyes) : ' Whither are we going ? ' All his inquiries into the original sentiments

64

of his contemporaries serve him at the same
time for his researches into the meaning and
end of life. He takes it very seriously indeed.
He is never humorous, nor even ironical or
flippant. He ignores the smile. He is anti-
Pagan and anti-Gallic. He has, what is
almost always the mark of a Christian education, a liking for chastity. You will find
often enough in him a vivid recollection of the
Catholic faith of his childhood. He is, as I
have said, as grave in the presence of love and
its dramas as M. Dumas the younger. And
that is why this disciple of Stendhal, that is to
say of the most detached of analysts, once expressed in the most eloquent of his studies such
an ardent sympathy for the author of *Visite
de Noces*. On the whole, Baudelairism, Renanism and Beylism are habits and tastes of his
mind, perhaps, also, premeditated acquisitions
of an artist who has made it his task to
reflect and carry within himself the soul of a
certain literary epoch. But in the depths of
his heart and of his being there is, I think, a
very painful concern about the moral life,
an impossibility of confining himself to curiosity and speculation. Armand de Querne

65

after his ' crime of love ' is precisely M. Paul
Bourget ; and de Querne is the Ryons of M.
Dumas the younger—with his wit left out.

IV

You will find all these characteristics of his
criticism in M. Paul Bourget's novels, perhaps with something added.

First of all, there is that particular form
of curiosity, that desire to have lived the most
elegant life (morally and physically) that is
known in his time, sometimes a certain dandy-
ism, something also of a rather narrow and
feminine delicacy. He loves ' modernity,' but
only when it is aristocratic. As a matter of
fact, it is neither among the people nor among
the lower middle-classes, but only among the
idle classes whose sensibilities are still refined by all the delicate things of life that
there could be found a species of love complex
enough and rich enough in the finer shades
to offer him material suited to his analytical
faculties. Moreover, an innate taste led him
towards this world, towards the life that is
lived around the Arc de Triomphe, and to-

wards the souls and bodies of the women who dwell there. Perhaps he has only confessed this taste with a touch of complacence. Some of his pages seem written by a novelist who has a weakness for London. There is a little fashionable Anglomania in his case. He has a very marked weakness for the fair foreigners who spend their winters in Paris. One of his first books, *Edel,* a melancholy and rather ingenuous poem, is above all a very modish poem. But it would be unjust and puerile to insist on this point.

The power of analysis, so remarkable in the *Essais,* is not less so in the novels. Nobody, I believe, since Madame de La Fayette, since Racine, since Marivaux, since Laclos, since Benjamin Constant, since Stendhal, has inferred with greater happiness, described with more exactness, linked together with more probability, or expounded with greater detail the feelings that a given person should experience in a given moral situation. At certain moments, and outside of the emotion which the drama itself can inspire, this assumes something of the special interest and appropriate beauty of a lesson in anatomy.

The pages in which M. Paul Bourget explains to us why the heroine of *Deuxième Amour* refuses a new experience, or describes the pure adolescent love with which Hubert Liauran loves Madame de Sauves, and how by a delightful reversal of parts Thérese treats him as if it were he who was yielding himself (*Cruelle Énigme*), or how, in *Crime d'Amour*, the frankness and innocence of Hélene Chazel turn against her and only provoke the distrust of Armand de Querne, or by what sentimental logic Hélene comes to stain herself in order to be avenged on the man who has not believed her and in order that he may believe in her at last . . . all those pages—and how many others !—are accomplished examples of living psychology. In truth, I do not believe that any writer, not even Stendhal, has shown superior penetration in the study of ' the passions of love.'

Let us quote a little, at hazard, and for the pleasure of doing so :

> ' Like all romantic women, Hélene occupied herself with the delicacy of the pleasures common to herself and her lover as with a sentimental anxiety. What ren-

ders a woman of this class completely unintelligible to a libertine is that he is accustomed to separate the things of pleasure from those of the heart, and to enjoy pleasure under humiliating conditions ; instead of which the romantic woman who is in love, not having known pleasure except when associated with the noblest exaltation, brings to her enjoyment the worship which she has for her moral emotions. Hélene came with an amorous piety, almost with a mystic idolatry, to the world of wild caresses and embraces.'

There are a hundred pages as good as this in M. Paul Bourget's three rather short novels and in his tales. That is a solid foundation for fame.

The danger is that a writer endowed with such an instrument of analysis may be tempted to use it with some indiscretion, and may sometimes dissect, with a rather excessive anatomical attention and display, states of soul that are fairly simple and fairly well known. The external apparatus of psychological research is not always perhaps, in the author of *Cruelle Énigme,* proportioned to its object. He has not the gift of modest analysis. He resembles, here and there, a too brilliant surgeon who would display and employ a whole case of instruments, a whole set of lances, saws, scissors, and pliers, in order to open an abscess in the cheek. For example, it seems to me that the remorse of the young girl in *L'Irréparable*, the jealousy of Hubert in *Cruelle Énigme*, are analysed at rather too great length, and that the display of these investigations is not justified by any discovery of importance. At times it becomes a mere exercise. M. Paul Bourget himself calls his last novel, *André Cornélis*, a ' plank of moral anatomy,' and he is only too right. The situation of that modern Hamlet, who is of so decided a character, and does not hesitate an instant as to his right, this situation is such that from the outset, granting the character of that personage, it implies his possession of only a small number of very simple feelings, continually repeated description of which becomes a little monotonous, and, moreover, we are not very greatly interested in what he experiences. For this situation is too extraordinary, too much out-

side all the probabilities of our life. Do I
know what I would do if by chance I discovered that when I was a child a man of honour
had killed my father, it being true also that
the murderer was loved by my mother and
was madly in love with her, that he had married her and made her perfectly happy, and
that, in addition, he was going to die in a
short time of a disease of the liver? Such
hypotheses find me absolutely unprepared.
In reality, I believe I would do nothing.
The subject ought to have been left to
Gaboriau, who would have expatiated very
little on the psychology of the new Hamlet,
and would have fastened upon its melodrama-
tic and judicial side. It seems to me that
instead of making André Cornélis so prodigiously energetic a fellow (which, moreover,
is not perhaps very compatible with the habits
of extreme analysis which he is at the same
time endowed with), I should have conceived
of him as a creature more uncertain than the
English Hamlet, and should, in addition,
have hampered him with doubts and hesita-
tions as to his right to murder. Except by a
mistake the modern Hamlet would not even

attempt to kill his stepfather—above all
when that stepfather is so charming an assas-
sin that one would like to find a gentler term
to apply to him. For one would say that,
contrary to Shakespeare, M. Bourget has endeavoured to make Claudius as little odious as
he could, and, on the other hand, to accumu-
late round Hamlet all the circumstances calculated to paralyse him, and to render action
impossible for him except by a miracle of
energy. For all these reasons *André Cornélis*
scarcely interests me save as a fine composition of ' applied psychology ' on a given subject. And if I must tell my whole mind (and
no longer solely in reference to *André Cornélis*),
M. Paul Bourget's psychology, which often
equals and even surpasses that of Benjamin
Constant and Stendhal, sometimes reminds
me of that of Madame de Souza or of Madame
de Duras—with much more embarrassment.
Note that even this is far from being contemptible.

But, happily, what puts M. Paul Bourget
in a place apart, what gives life to his analyses, what, when they are profound, renders
them tragic as well, is the feeling which we

have already found at the basis of his *Essais*
—a concern about moral life. His novels
(*André Cornélis* excepted) are dramas of conscience, stories of scruples, of remorse, of re-
pentance, of expiations and purifications.
Irréparable is the story of a young girl who
dies through the memory of a stain. *Deuxième
Amour* is the story of a woman who, having
been deceived, thinks she has no right to begin a fresh experience of love. *Cruelle Énigme*,
this title alone makes the book that bears it
a Christian novel ; for, whether Thérese de-
ceives Hubert whilst loving him, or whether
Hubert returns to Thérese whilst despising
her, in brief, whether the flesh is stronger than
the spirit, this is certainly not an ' enigma ' for
the disciples of Béranger or even for those of
the grave Lucretius. M. Paul Bourget only
finds the servitudes of the flesh ' enigmatic '
because he judges them to be base and
humiliating, and he only judges them thus
because at the bottom of his heart he is a
Christian.

Similarly, in *Crime d'Amour*, what de
Querne does is only ' a crime ' in the eyes of a
man who believes in moral responsibility and

in the worth of souls. Armand de Querne, his heart withered by a motherless childhood, by the immorality of the events among which he has grown up, and, lastly, by the abuse of analysis, has taken Hélene without being able to love her and without believing in the young woman's purity. Hélene, when abandoned, revenges herself upon him by a voluntary act of impurity. It is therefore he who has ruined her. This idea stirs in him a great distress, a terrible remorse, and, finally, an immense pity for universal human suffering. He finds Hélene again ; he asks her pardon, and she pardons him. She also has been led back to a Christian conception of life by the spectacle of another's (her husband's) suffering. This novel is therefore, upon the whole, a story of expiation, the story of two souls purified by pain.

Crime d'Amour seems to me to be M. Bourget's masterpiece up to the present, and one of the finest novels that have been written within the past twenty years ; for I see none other in which one finds at once so great a power of analysis and so much emotion, none which presents so faithful a mirror of

their own souls to the most distinguished of
spirits among us. How many of us there are
who recognize themselves (some more, some
less) in Armand de Querne! Who has not
known that incapacity to love, to love absolutely and with one's whole being, to love
otherwise than from desire and curiosity?
Who has not experienced that incapacity,
whether it brings enjoyment (for at least it
leaves us tranquil and composed, and it has
airs of intellectual distinction), or whether,
at certain moments, it brings suffering, when
one feels the emptiness of a sceptical, detached, and merely curious life, and how good
it would be to love, and how one can do ill
by not loving? But this anxiety is already
the beginning of moral redemption, it is the
sign that all virtue is not dead in us. What do
I say? It is perhaps the sign of a more
religious, more largely human power of loving,
than that of the great lovers. In any case,
it is this which distinguishes Armand de
Querne from those who will never love, from
heartless libertines and eager *virtuosi* of love,
from the Valmonts and the Lovelaces ; and
it is this that makes him our brother. Since

he suffers because he does not love he is therefore still able to love !

The first time that I read *Crime d'Amour* I made a mistake about it. I said to myself : ' What a feeble libertine this man is who imagines himself to be so strong ! He cannot love Hélene because he does not believe her when she tells him that he is her first lover ; but, as he knows women so well, he ought to feel that this one is telling the truth ! He ought to believe her, and even whilst believing her, not be able to love her—and not suffer but from this cause ! ' But I understood the book ill. De Querne is not Valmont. He is still less so than M. Paul Bourget wished. In his weakness and in his apparent sterility he retains a basis of goodness and tenderness by which ' salvation ' will come to him. But for that end it is necessary for him to have mistaken Hélene, it is necessary for her to have ruined herself through him ; it is necessary for him to have been cruel and unjust without wishing to be so. This is necessary, in order that some day he may be seized by terror and touched to the depth of his heart before the evil he has done, and that he may feel the Christian awakening within him, and that the question of moral responsibility and others of the same sort may again confront him, and that, as by a flash of lightning, he may see all the wretchedness of life— and all its mystery. Armand de Querne is the man of to-day, a man who has conceived and experienced all the states of soul analysed in the *Essais*, and sums up in his person the whole moral and intellectual distinction that has been erected by the effort of the last two generations. This man of to-day presents a singular combination of scientific temper, refined and melancholy sensuality, moral anxiety, tender compassion, returning religious feeling, inclination towards mysticism, towards an explanation of the world by means of something that is inaccessible and extra-natural. The end of *Crime d'Amour* is as mystic as a Russian novel. But to that point of view to which the Russian novelists have been led by the spontaneous movement of their religious and dreaming souls, by the study of simple hearts, and by the sight of infinite sufferings and infinite resignations, we have reached, I think, by the bankruptcy of analysis and criticism, by the feeling of void that they make in us, and of the enormous unexplained burden that they leave in the world. For these or other reasons, it seems that a tenderness of the human soul is in process of being produced at this century's end, and that we may soon—who knows ?— witness an awakening of the Gospel.

It is this tenderness, made up of serious meditation, sadness, and pity, that gives so much value to M. Paul Bourget's novels. It was this which early communicated so much sweetness to the poems of his youth (*La Vie Inquiète* and *Aveux*).

I do not conclude. M. Paul Bourget is young enough to develop further and to give us something that we do not expect. Let him continue to charm us, to touch us, and to make us reflect ; let him continue to be eloquent, grave and languid, to draw for us exquisite figures of women (like Thérese de Sauves, Hélene Chazel, the two Marie-Alices, or like Hubert Liauran, that sweet little girl) ; and to study the dramas of conscience in love. And if it were not indiscreet and useless to form wishes, I should add let him also propound

78

to us, if such is his pleasure, cases of the psychology of the passions, but let him not confine himself to them ; he would soon be condemned to repeat himself a little. Besides, do the tragedies of love occupy the whole of life ? Look, I pray you, within you and around you : you will see that there is something else in the world. M. Paul Bourget has felt it in *André Cornélis* ; but it is not ' planks of pure anatomy,' particularly of such exceptional anatomy, that we ask from him. Let him bid defiance to his eternal Stendhal, and even a little to M. Taine. Let him apply to the analysis of other passions than those of love, to the study of other situations than those in which we can find ourselves confronted by woman, his marvellous gifts as a psychologist who is also a moralist. And, lastly, let him make the universe of his novels as large as that of his *Essais*. I ask nothing more from this young sage, the prince of youth—of the youth of a very old century.

ERNEST RENAN

No writer, perhaps, has so much occupied, haunted, disturbed or delighted the more fastidious among his contemporaries. Whether we yield to or resist his attraction, none has more engrossed thought, nor fixed himself upon it so closely. This great sceptic has amongst the youth of to-day fervent admirers such as an apostle and a doctrinal teacher would have.

Parisians will excuse the ignorance and ingenuousness of a provincial who has recently come up from his province, who is curious to see famous men and who continues to make discoveries. I am a little like those worthy Spaniards who came from the end of Iberia in order to see Titus Livius, ' seeking in Rome something other than Rome itself.' The feeling that brought them was natural and touching, childish if you will, that is to say, doubly human. In this spirit I went to the Collège de France, into the little hall of Semitic studies.

I

To what purpose, however ? Is it not by their books and by their books alone that we know writers, and above all, philosophers and critics, those who directly deliver to us their thought, their conception of the world, and hence their whole soul. What can the features of their countenances or the sounds of their voices add to the knowledge we have of them ? What matters how their noses are formed ? And whether they happen to be ill-shaped or shaped like everybody else ?

But no, we want to know. How many pious young people have made their pilgrimage to the Avenue d'Eylau in order there to contemplate the solemn mummy of the god who survives himself ! Luckily, people see what they wish when they look with the eyes of faith, and poor humanity, whatever it may do, has an irreducible bump of veneration.

Moreover, it is not certain that love is incompatible with at least a small remnant of the critical sense. Have you noticed this? When one is smitten, thoroughly and completely smitten, one can nevertheless seize very clearly on the faults and infirmities of what our fathers used to call the loved object, and, as one is pained at not seeing it perfect and one becomes exasperated (not against it), this pity and this exasperation redouble our tenderness. We wish to forget and we hide from it (though we know it well) whatever can be disagreeable in it, and this delicate care keeps our love on the alert and draws it closer to us by making it more meritorious and giving it the appearance of a challenge. Therefore so far from extinguishing it, criticism can give fresh food to passion.

Conclusion : it is only with tepid persons that great artists lose by being seen close at hand ; but this test cannot impair them in the eyes of him who is truly captivated. And they gain by being better known without being the less loved.

II

This is, I think, the case with M. Renan. One thing used to worry me. Is this extraordinary man really melancholy or is he lighthearted ? We may hesitate if we confine ourselves to his books. For if he almost always ends in a tone of declared optimism, it is none the less true that his conception of the world and of history, his ideas on contemporary society and on the future, lend themselves quite as easily to saddening conclusions. The old phrase, ' All is vanity,' so often and so richly commented upon by him, can quite as well have for its complement, ' What good is life ? ' as ' Let us drink, my brothers, and let us keep joyful.' That the end of the universe is profoundly hidden from us ; that this world has all the appearance of a spectacle given to himself by a God who doubtless does not exist, but who shall exist and who is in process of creating himself ; that virtue is a deception for the individual, but that, however, it is elegant to be virtuous while knowing that we are duped ; that art, poetry, and even virtue are pretty things, but that their time will soon be over, and that the

world must one day be ruled by the Academy
of Sciences, etc.—all this is amusing on the
one hand, and desolating on the other. It
was by dismal arguments that, in his little
speech at Tréguier, M. Renan advised his
contemporaries to be joyous. Indeed his
light-heartedness on that day seemed the
light-heartedness of a very distinguished and
very erudite undertaker's mute.

M. Sarcey, who looks at things in the lump
and who always goes straight to the point,
settles the matter by calling M. Renan a
' jester,' a superior and transcendental jester.
Yes, indeed! M. Renan scoffs at us. But
does he always scoff, and up to what point
does he scoff? And, moreover, there are
' jesters ' who are very much to be pitied.
The scoffer often suffers and dies of his own
irony. Once again, is this sage light-hearted
or is he sad? The impression left by the
reading of his works is complex and ambiguous. We are greatly amused ; we are pleased
with ourselves for having understood them ;
but at the same time we feel ourselves
troubled, disconcerted, detached from all
positive belief, contemptuous of the crowd,

superior to the ordinary and vulgar conception of duty, and as it were stiffened in an ironical attitude towards foolish reality. The magician's pride, passing into simple-minded people like ourselves, becomes coarser and duller. And how could he be light-hearted when shortly after reading him we are so sad ?

Let us come then and see and hear him. The tones of his voice, the expression of his countenance and of his whole mortal envelope will doubtless tell us what we want to find out. What do we risk ? He will not suspect that we are there ; in us he will only notice the faces of a few curious persons ; he will not overwhelm us with his ecclesiastical politeness before which men of wit and imbeciles are alike equal ; he will not know that we are simpletons, and he will not make us feel that we are intruders.

I have proved this for myself. And I know what I wished to know. M. Renan is light-hearted, very light-hearted, and, what is more, he is comically light-hearted.

III

There is nothing particularly noticeable about those present at his course of lectures. We see there many old gentlemen who look like all other old gentlemen, some students, some ladies, a few Englishwomen who come because M. Renan is one of the ' sights' of Paris.

He enters ; there is applause. He returns thanks with a little nod, smiling in a good-natured manner. He is thick-set, short, fat, and fresh-complexioned ; with large features, long grey hair, a large nose, a shrewd mouth ; besides, he is quite round, and moves bolt upright, with his large head planted on his shoulders. He has the air of a man who is satisfied with life, and he cheerfully expounds to us the formation of that historic *Corpus* which includes the Pentateuch and the Book of Joshua, and which should be more correctly called the Hexateuch.

He explains how this *Torah* was at first written in two forms almost at the same time and how in the present redaction we can see the two primitive redactions, the Jehovist and the Elohist ; that therefore there were

86

two types of sacred history as there were afterwards two Talmuds, that of Babylon and that of Jerusalem ; that the fusion of the two narratives took place probably under Hezekiah, that is to say, in the time of Isaiah, after the destruction of the Northern Kingdom ; that the Pentateuch was then formed with the omission of Deuteronomy and Leviticus ; that Deuteronomy was added to it in the time of Josiah, and Leviticus a little later.

His exposition is clear, simple, and animated. His voice is a little husky, a little unctuous, his diction very measured and sustained, his gestures familiar and almost excessive. As for the form, it has not the least touch of studied care or even the least elegance ; it shows nothing of the grace or refinement of his written style. He speaks to make himself understood, that is all ; and he follows the line of least resistance. He does not construct ' binding-links.' He expresses himself exactly as if he were sitting by the fireside with ' Oh's ' and ' Ah's ' and ' Entirely's ' and ' Not at all's.' Like all professors, he has two or three words or phrases which he often employs. He makes

great use of ' in some way or other,' a prudent
expression, and he is ready with ' do not
doubt,' which is perhaps the gentlest formula
of affirmation, for it implicitly admits the
right to doubt. I give a few specimens of his
manner. I hope they will amuse, for they
are exactly life-like.

In reference to the redaction of the Torah,
which was made without noise, which has
remained anonymous, of which we do not even
know the precise date because all that is
written in it was already known, already
existed in tradition :

' How different this is, is it not ?—from
what happens in our own days ! The
redaction of a code, of a legislation, we
would discuss it publicly, the newspapers
would speak of it, it would be an event.
Well, the redaction of the Pentateuch
was not an event at all ! '

In reference to Oriental historians compared
with those of the West :

' Among the Greeks, among the Romans, history is a Muse. Oh ! they are
artists those Greeks and those Romans !
Livy, for example, performs a work of

art ; he digests his documents and assimilates them so thoroughly that we no longer distinguish them. Thus we can never criticize him by comparing him with himself ; his art effaces the traces of his mistakes. Well ! you have not this in the East ; oh ! no, you have not this ! In the East, nothing but compilers ; they juxtapose, mingle, pile up. They devour anterior documents, they do not digest them. What they devour remains entire in their stomach ; you can take out the morsels.'

In reference to the date of Leviticus :

' Ah ! I compliment those who are sure of these matters. The best thing is to affirm nothing, or to change one's opinion from time to time. In this way one has at least the chance of being right once.'

In reference to the Levites :

' Oh ! Levitism was not always what it was in the time of Josiah. In the early days, as worship was very complicated, there was need of a class of sacristans, very powerful and knowing their business very well. But Levitism organized into a sacerdotal body belongs to the epoch of the reconstruction of the Temple.'

Finally, I gather up a few chance phrases : ' Well, yes ! this is complicated, but it is not yet complicated enough.'—' Has this redaction of Leviticus been finished ? No, it has come to an end.'—' Ah ! Deuteronomy is perfect. It forms a whole. It has not been cut.'

I am here afraid of doing M. Renan an injustice under pretext of reproducing exactly his living words. I feel very deeply that, detached from the person of the orator, from all that accompanies them, relieves and saves them, these rather abrupt fragments may take on an almost grotesque appearance. They make us think of some exegetical Labiche, of Scripture criticism expounded by L'héritier, in front of the prompter's box, in some fantastic monologue. Well ! my loyalty compels me to warn the reader that it is not this. Assuredly, I do not think that Ramus, Vatable, or Budé lectured in this tone ; and it is a sign of the times that this absence of all solemnity and this pleasant good-nature

are to be found in the most exalted chairs of
the Collège de France. But it is only just to
add that M. Renan sticks to good-nature.
Formalities of phrasing or even of pronuncia-
tion are saved by the cordiality of his tone
and the good grace of his smile. The ' Oh's,'
the ' Ah's,' the ' Not at all,' the ' I don't
know ' and the ' That's the truth ' can be
laughable or vulgar or simply attractive.
M. Renan's ' carelessnesses ' belong to the
latter category. He chats, that is all, to a good
and very faithful old audience with whom he
feels at his ease.

You now seize the tone, the accent, the gait
of these lectures. They are something very
living. M. Renan seems to take a prodigious
interest in what he explains, and to amuse
himself enormously. Do not believe what he
says somewhere of historical sciences, of ' those
poor little conjectural sciences.' He loves
them, whatever he may say, and he finds them
entertaining. No one has ever seen so jovial
an exegete. He experiences a visible pleasure
in praising or contradicting MM. Reuss, Graff,
Kuenen, Wellhausen, very great men, but self-
willed or credulous. The Jehovist and the

Elohist, mixed up 'like two packs of cards,' are very amusing to disentangle. And when the sly Hilkiah, the high priest, has just said : ' I have found the book of the law in the house of the Lord,' and gives us in this way the exact date of Deuteronomy, M. Renan is beside himself with joy.

But it is especially when he meets (without looking for it) some piece of drollery that you ought to see him ! His powerful head, leaning on one shoulder and thrown backwards, becomes lit up and radiant ; his eyes gleam, and there is a priceless contrast between the shrewd, half-open mouth which gives a glimpse of his very small teeth, and the luxuriant, episcopal, largely and even coarsely moulded jaws and chaps. It makes us think of those succulent faces, drawn with such marvellous relief, which Gustave Doré has sprinkled among his illustrations of Rabelais or the *Contes Drolatiques*, and the very sight of which makes one burst into laughter. Or rather, one feels in it a whole ironical poem, a very subtle and alert spirit entangled in too much matter, which accommodates itself to it, and even turns it to good account by radiating

the malice of its smile from all points of that
mask, as if to be able to scoff with a huger
countenance were to scoff better and in the
most complete manner possible !

All the same, one feels a disappointment,
if not a deception. M. Renan has not at all
the appearance that his books and his life
ought to have given him. In that face,
which one imagined to be moulded by transcendental scepticism, one rather discerns the
imprint of the thumb of " Béranger's Theol-
ogy," of which he has made such delightful
fun. I imagine that an artist in oratorical
movements would have here a fine oppor-
tunity for the exercise of his talent.

' This man,' he would say, ' has passed
through the most terrible moral crisis that a
soul can traverse. He was forced, at twenty
years of age and in conditions that rendered
the choice particularly painful and dramatic,
to choose between faith and knowledge, to
break the strongest and gentlest bonds, and,
as he was more pledged than most people, the
rupture has doubtless been all the greater.
And he is light-hearted !

' Because of a less intimate rupture (for

perhaps he was only a rhetorician), Lammennais died in final despair. Because of much less than that, the frank Jouffroy remained incurably sad. Because of less still, not because he doubted, but only because he feared he might doubt, Pascal went mad. And M. Renan is light-hearted !

' Admit even that he had changed his faith ; he could have the serenity which strong conviction often gives. But this philosopher has kept the imagination of a Catholic. He still loves what he has denied. He has remained a priest ; he gives to negation itself a mystic Christian turn. His brain is a disaffected cathedral.[1] It is filled with hay, or lectures are given in it : but it is always a church. And he laughs ! he is glad ! he is light-hearted !

' This man has spent twenty years of his life studying the most considerable and most mysterious event in history. He has seen how religions are born ; he has penetrated into the depths of the consciences of simple and visionary men ; he has seen how men must be unhappy in order to frame dreams,

[1] The phrase is M. Alphonse Daudet's.

and how simple-minded they must be in order to console themselves by doing so. And he is light-hearted !

' This man, in the *Lettre à M. Berthelot*, has magnificently traced the formidable and established programme that faces the modest inventory of what science has done. On that day he felt, and he communicated to us, the sensation of the infinite. He has felt, better than any one else, how vain are our efforts and how indecipherable is our destiny. And he is light-hearted !

' This man, having to speak lately of that poor Amiel who suffered so much from his thoughts, who died slowly of the malady of metaphysics, amused himself by maintaining, with the insolence of a page-boy, with the elusive logic of a woman, and with some pretty flips directed towards God, that this world is not, after all, so sad for those who do not take it too seriously, that there are a thousand ways of being happy, and that those to whom it has not been given " to work out their salvation " by virtue or by science can do so by means of travel, women, sport, or drink. (Perhaps I am not doing justice to his thought by translating it. So much the worse ! Why has he subtleties that are bound up with the arrangement of the words ?) I know well that pessimism, in spite of its airs, is not a philosophy, and is only an unreasonable feeling born of an incomplete view of things ; but, all the same, one encounters very impertinent optimists ! What ! this sage himself admitted, a little before, that, whatever one may say, there exist useless and inexplicable sufferings ; the great cry of universal pain mounted to his ears in spite of himself. And immediately afterwards he is light-hearted ! Woe to those who laugh ! as the Scripture says. I have already heard that laugh in the *Odyssey* ; it is the involuntary and mournful laugh of the suitors who are about to die.

' No, no, M. Renan has no right to be light-hearted. He can only be so by the most audacious or the blindest inconsistency. As Macbeth murdered sleep, so M. Renan, twenty times, a hundred times, in each of his books has killed joy, has killed action, has killed the peace of the soul and the security of the moral life. To practise virtue with the mental reservation that perhaps the virtuous man is a fool ; to construct for oneself " a double-edged wisdom " ; to say to oneself that " we owe virtue to the Eternal, but that, as a personal equivalent, we have a right to join irony to it ; that by this means we return jest for jest," etc., all this is very pretty, very pretty. It is delightful and absurd reasoning, and the " good God," who is conceived of as a sort of superannuated Greek who loads the dice, is a most amusing invention. But never to do good with simplicity, to do it only elegantly and with the show of a trickster, to put so much wit in being good when you happen to be so, to bring always to the practise of virtue the distrust and sagacity of a gentleman who is not to be caught napping and who is a dupe only because he wishes—does not that—supposing it is possible—seem to you to be lamentable ? To say that God does not exist, but that perhaps He will exist some day, and that He will be the consciousness of the universe when the universe becomes conscious ; to say, besides, that " God is already good, that He is not yet almighty, but that doubtless He will be so some day " ; that " immortality is not a gift inherent in man,

97

a consequence of his nature, but doubtless a
gift reserved by the Being, become absolute,
perfect, omniscient, and almighty, for those
who shall have contributed to his development " ; " that, moreover, there are almost
an equal number of chances that the contrary
is true," and " that a complete obscurity
conceals from us the ends of universe "—are
not these, for any one who examines them
thoroughly, fine and sound negations enveloped in subtle mockery ?   Let us not fear
to be regarded as coarse and positive spirits,
ignorant of the finer shades.   There are no
finer shades that remain.   To doubt and
banter in this way is simply to deny ; and
this nihilism, however elegant it is, can only
be an abyss of black melancholy and despair.
Notice that I do not dispute the truth of this
philosophy (that is not my business) ; I only
testify to its profound sadness.   Nothing,
nothing, there is nothing except phenomena.
M. Renan does not recoil from any of the
consequences of his thought.   He has a surprising phrase in which " to work out one's
salvation " becomes exactly synonymous with
" taking one's pleasure wherever one finds

it," and in which he admits the existence of saints of lewdness, of morphia, and of alcohol. And with all this, he is light-hearted ! How can he manage it ? '

Somebody could answer :

' You are easily astonished, my simple-minded friend. You might as well say : " This man is a man, and he has the audacity to be light-hearted ! " And do not protest that his cheerfulness is sinister, for I would show you that it is heroic. This sage has had an austere youth ; he recognized after thirty years of study that that very austerity was a vanity, that he has been his own dupe, that it is the simple and the frivolous who are right, but that to-day he no longer has time to eat his share of the cake. He knows this, he has said so a hundred times, yet he is cheerful. It is admirable ! '

Well, no. I suspect this cheerfulness of being neither sinister nor heroic. It remains that it is natural, and that M. Renan satisfies himself with maintaining it by all that he knows of men and things. And that is certainly permissible ; for if this world is distressing as an enigma, it is still amusing enough as a spectacle.

One can push the explanation further There is no reason why the most extreme Pyrrhonist or disbeliever should not be a cheerful man, and this even supposing that negation or universal doubt implies a view of the world and of human life which is necessarily and irremediably sad, a fact which has not been demonstrated. In any case, this would only be true of men of refined culture and tender hearts, for there is nothing to prevent scoundrels from being complete disbelievers and yet jolly fellows. For in reality it is not necessary to be a blackguard in order to be gay with a sad philosophy. One is a sceptic, a pessimist, or a nihilist when one thinks of it ; the rest of the time (and this rest is almost all life), well, one lives, one comes and goes, one travels, one has one's work, one's pleasures, one's little occupations of all sorts. You remember what Pascal says of ' the metaphysical proofs of God,' those demonstrations which strike one only during the moment that one lays hold of them ; an hour afterwards, they are forgotten. It is thus very possible for there to be a contrast between a man's character and his ideas, above all if he is very cultivated. ' Judgment,' says Montaigne, ' holds in me a magistral seat. . . . It allows my appetites to go their own way. . . . *It does its work apart.*' Why should it not also do its work apart in the deceptive author of the *Dialogues Philosophiques* ? Let us therefore try and see where and how he can be happy.

First of all, his optimism is a decision openly proclaimed on every occasion, and even without occasion, and at the most unexpected moments. He is happy because he wishes to be happy ; which is still the best manner that has been found of being so. He gives in this an example which many of his contemporaries ought to follow. By force of pitying ourselves, we become really unhappy. The best remedy for pain is perhaps to deny it as much as one can. A sensibility invades us, very human, very generous even, but also very dangerous. We must act without bewailing, and aid our neighbour without bathing him in tears. I do not know, but perhaps ' poor people ' have become less happy since they have been given more pity. Their misery was great formerly, and yet I believe it was less to be pitied precisely because less pity was given to it.

I am willing, moreover, to grant to feeble souls that to wish for happiness is not always sufficient to produce it. Life, on the whole, has not served M. Renan too ill, has aided him tolerably well to stick to his opinion ; and, at the end of his *Souvenirs,* he gracefully gives thanks for this to the obscure ' first cause.' All his dreams have been realized. He is a member of both Academies ; he is a trustee of the Collège de France ; he has been loved, he tells us, by the three women whose love mattered to him, his sister, his wife, and his daughter ; finally, he has a comfortable competence, not in landed property, which is too material and binding a thing, but in stocks and preference shares, light things which suit him better, being a species of fiction and even of pretty fiction. He has rheumatism. But he employs his coquetry to prevent us from noticing it, and then he has not got it always. His greatest sorrow has been the loss of his sister, Henriette ; but he has at least been

spared the sight of her long and terrible
death-bed, for he himself was very ill at that
moment. She departed when her work was
done and when her brother had hardly any
further need of her. And who knows whether
the memory of that accomplished person is
not as sweet as her presence would be to-day?
And then her death has inspired him with such
fine, such tender, such harmonious pages!
Furthermore, if it is true that happiness is
often the recompense of simple hearts, it
seems to me that it is not in the nature of a
superior intelligence and all that it brings
with it to prevent itself from being happy.
It is to men what great beauty is to women.
A truly beautiful woman enjoys her beauty
continually, she cannot forget it for a moment,
she reads it in all eyes. With it life is endur-
able, or it quickly becomes so again, unless in
the case of a passionate maddened woman, a
bungler with happiness, for such persons
exist. M. Renan feels himself sovereignly
intelligent, just as Cleopatra found herself
sovereignly beautiful. He has the pleasures
of extreme celebrity, which are almost continual, and are not so much to be despised,

at least so I imagine. His fame smiles on him in every glance. He feels himself superior to almost all his contemporaries by the quantity of things he understands, by the interpretation which he gives to them, and by the subtleties of that interpretation. He feels himself the inventor of a certain very refined philosophy, of a certain way of conceiving of the world and of taking hold of life, and he discovers all around him the influence exerted on many souls by his aristocratic theories. (I do not speak of the regular and assured joys of daily work, of the pleasures of research, and sometimes of discovery.) M. Renan enjoys his own genius and his own wit. M. Renan is the first to enjoy Renanism.

It would be interesting—and also useless—to make out a list of M. Renan's contradictions. His God by turns exists or does not exist, is personal or impersonal. The immortality of which he sometimes dreams is by turns individual and collective. He believes and he does not believe in progress. His thought is sad and his mind is humorous. He loves historical science and he despises it.

He is piously impious. He is very chaste, and he often calls up sensual images. He is a mystic and he is a cynical jester. He has moods of ingenuousness and of inextricable malice. He is a Breton and a Gascon. He is an artist, and yet his style is the least plastic that it is possible to see. This style seems to be precise, and in reality it flows like water through the fingers. Often the thought is clear and the expression obscure, unless it be the contrary. Under an appearance of connectedness there are incredible and sudden changes in the ideas, and there are continual abuses of words, imperceptible evasions, sometimes delightful nonsense. He denies at the same time as he affirms. He is so preoccupied with not being the dupe of his own thought that he cannot advance anything in the least serious without smiling and jesting immediately afterwards. A moment later he has the air of not believing in his own affirmations, or, on the other hand, one would say that he allows himself to be taken in by his own ironical paradoxes. But does he himself know where his irony begins and ends ? His exoteric opinions are so jumbled up with the

' thoughts at the back of his head,' that I think he himself no longer finds his way among them and is lost before us in the mystery of these ' fine shades.'

All the fairies gave rich presents to the little Armorican. They gave him genius, imagination, subtlety, perseverance, cheerfulness, kindness. The fairy, Irony, came in her turn, and said to him : ' I bring you a charming gift ; but I bring it to you in such abundance that it will invade and alter all the others. You will be loved ; but as people will always be afraid of passing for fools in your eyes, they will not dare to tell you. You will ridicule men, the universe, and God, you will ridicule yourself, and you will end by losing regard and fondness for truth. You will mingle irony with the gravest thoughts, with the most natural and the best actions, and irony will render all your writings infinitely seductive, but inconsistent and fragile. In return, never will anybody be so much amused as you at being in the world.' Thus spoke the fairy, and, upon the whole, she was a good enough person. If M. Renan is an enigma, M. Renan is the first to enjoy the riddle, and perhaps he studies it in order to complicate it more.

Fourteen years ago, he wrote : ' This universe is a spectacle which God has given to himself ; let us help on the intentions of the great choragus by contributing to render the spectacle a brilliant and as varied as possible.' We must do the author of the *Vie de Jésus* this justice, that he agreeably helps on ' the intentions of the great choragus ' ! He is certainly one of the most original and ingenious ' godfathers ' in the eternal land of fairy. Shall we reproach him for amusing himself whilst he amuses the Divine impresario ? That would be ingratitude, for we also enjoy the comedy in our own little measure ; and truly the world would be a duller place if M. Renan was not in it.

EMILE ZOLA

THERE are some writers and artists whose intimate, delicate, subtle charm is very difficult to seize upon and fix in a formula. There are also some whose talent is a very rich amalgam, a happy equilibrium of contrary qualities; and it is not very easy to seize upon these latter either, or to define them with precision. But there are others in whom some one faculty is strongly predominant, in a brutal and extravagant manner, some inclination, some mania; they are a species of powerful, simple, and clear monsters, whose prominent features it is pleasant to draw in bold outlines. In their case we can do something that may be called criticizing in fresco.

M. Emile Zola is one of these vigorous 'extremists,' especially since *L'Assommoir*. But as it seems that he has but little knowledge of himself, as he has done all that he can to give the public an absolutely false idea of his work and talent, it is perhaps well, before seeking what he is, to say what he is not.

I

M. Zola is not a man of critical feeling, although he has written *Le Roman Expéri-mental*, or rather because he has written it ; and M. Zola is not a veracious novelist, although that is his great claim.

It is impossible to imagine a more surprising equivocation, or one sustained and developed at greater length, than that which forms the basis of his volume on the *Roman Expéri-mental*. But there has been enough ridicule of that assimilation of a novel with a chemical experiment to make it useless to dwell upon it. It remains that, for M. Zola, the novel *ought* to cling more closely to reality than is possible. If this be advice, it is good but commonplace. If it be a dogma, we rise up against it and claim the liberty of art. If M. Zola thinks that he preaches by example, he is mistaken.

We are quite ready to recognize with M. Zola that many things in romanticism have grown old and appear ridiculous ; that the works which interest us most to-day are those that issue from the observation of men as they are, dragging a body about with them, living in conditions and in an ' environment ' whose influence they undergo. But M. Zola also knows well that the artist, in order to bring his models into the novel or on to the stage, is *forced* to choose, to retain only the expressive features of reality, and to arrange them in such a manner as to bring into relief the dominant character either of an environment or of a person. And then that is everything. What models ought one to take ? To what degree ought one to choose, and therefore to curtail ? This is a matter of taste and temperament. There are no laws for it ; he who proclaims them is a false prophet. Art, even naturalist art, is a transformation of reality ; by what right do you fix limits which it must not pass ? Tell me why must I be only moderately pleased by *Indiana* or even by *Julia de Trécœur* and *Méta Holdenis*. And what is this strange and pedantic tyranny which busies itself with ruling over my pleasures ? Let us enlarge our sympathies (M. Zola himself will gain by this), and let us allow everything to the artist, except to be mediocre and tiresome.

I will even allow him, when he groups his recollections, to imagine characters of whom reality presents no models, provided that those characters have unity and imitate men of flesh and bone in the particular logic that presides over their actions. I admit it without shame, I still love Lélia, I adore Consuelo, and I even put up with George Sand's workmen ; they have a sort of truth, and express a part of the ideas and passions of their time.

Thus M. Zola, under colour of literary criticism, has never done more than erect his own personal taste into a principle ; and this is a mark neither of a free nor of a liberal mind. And, unhappily, he has done it without grace, with an air of imperturbability, in the form of commandments to the youth of France. In this way he has irritated a number of worthy people, and has supplied them with such good reasons for not understanding him that they are very much to be excused for having used them. For this is what has happened. On the one hand, these worthy people have treated M. Zola's theories as absurd ; but at the same time they have affected to take them literally, and they have pleased themselves by showing that those theories have not been applied in his novels. They have, therefore, condemned the novels for not having observed rules which they themselves had just condemned. They have said, for example : ' Nana is not much like the courtesans one knows ; your middle-class people in *Pot-Bouille* are still less like ordinary middle-class folk ; moreover, your books are full of filth, and the proportion of what is ignoble in them is certainly greater than it is in real life ; therefore, they are not of the slightest value.' In brief, they have employed against M. Zola arms with which he himself has supplied them, and they want to make him bear the penalty of the theories which he has dinned into our ears.

This is, perhaps, fair war ; but it is not just criticism, for M. Zola's novels could run contrary to his doctrines and none the less be fine works. I should like, therefore, to defend him (without asking his permission to do so) both against his ' detractors ' and against his own illusions. ' It is false,' they shout at him, ' and it is squalid into the bargain.' I should like candidly to show that if M. Zola's pictures

are far-fetched and conceived according to a
system, it is through this that they are imposing, and that if they are often horrible, perhaps
they are horrible with some force, some
grandeur, and some poetry.

M. Zola is not a critic, and he is not a
' naturalist ' novelist in the sense in which he
means. But M. Zola is an epic poet and a
pessimist poet. And that is especially evident
in his latest novels.

I mean by a poet a writer who, by virtue of
an idea or in view of an ideal, notably transforms reality, and makes it live when it has
thus been modified. By this reckoning many
novelists and dramatic authors are poets ; but
what is interesting is that M. Zola denies it,
though he is more of one than anybody else.

If you compare M. Daudet with M. Zola, you
will see that M. Daudet is the naturalistic
novelist, not M. Zola ; that it is the author of
Nabab who begins with the observation of
reality, and is, as it were, possessed by it,
while the author of *L'Assommoir* only consults
it when his plan has been formed, and then
summarily and with preconceived ideas. The
one lays hold of real and almost always un-

usual personages, then looks for an action which binds them together and which is, at the same time, the natural development of the character or passions of his principal actors. The other wishes to paint a class, a group, which he knows in the mass, and which he represents to himself in a particular manner before making any special study ; he afterwards imagines a very simple and very broad drama in which masses can be moved and very general types fully shown. Thus M. Zola invents far more than he observes ; he is a true poet if we take the word in its etymological sense, which is a little crude—and an idealist poet if we give the word the reverse of its habitual meaning. Let us see then what sort of bold simplification this poet applies to the painting of men, things, and their surroundings, and we shall not be far from knowing him in his entirety.

II

When he was quite young, in his *Contes à Ninon*, M. Zola showed but a moderate fondness for the ' real truth,' and willingly indulged in some caprices of a rather insipid

poetry. He had certainly nothing of the
' experimenter ' in him. But he already
lacked wit and gaiety, and here and there he
showed himself to be a vigorous describer of
concrete things by means of an unwearied
accumulation of details.

Now that he has found his way and his
material, he appears to us, more and more, as
the sad and brutal poet of blind instincts,
coarse passions, carnal loves, and the base and
repugnant sides of human nature. What
interests him in man is above all the animal,
and in each human type the particular animal
which this type contains. It is this which he
loves to show, and it is the remainder which he
eliminates, in contradiction to properly idealist novelists. Eugène Delacroix used to say
that every human face, by a bold simplification of the features, by the exaggeration of
some and the reduction of others, can be
reduced to the face of an animal. It is quite
in this way that M. Zola simplifies souls.

Nana presents a striking example of this
simplification. What is she but the most
general, and consequently the least inviting,
a priori conception of the courtesan ? Nana

is not a Manon Lescaut or a Marguerite Gautier, nor is she a Madame Marneffe nor an Olympe Taverny. Nana is a beautiful animal with a magnificent and unwholesome body, stupid, without grace and without heart, neither evil nor good, irresistible by the sole power of her sex. She is the ' earthly Venus ' with ' coarse vulgar limbs.' She is woman reduced to her simplest and crudest expression. And see how by this the author escapes the reproach of intentional obscenity. Having conceived of his heroine in this way, he was condemned by the logic of things to write the book he has written ; being neither intellectual, nor evil, nor passionate, Nana could only be from head to heel—what she is. And to make her alive, to explain the sort of attraction which she exercises on men, the conscientious artist was obliged to plunge into the details which you know. Add that it was hardly possible for there to be any dramatic interest or progress in those crude adventures of the flesh. The caprices of her senses do not mark the phases of a development or of an internal toil. Nana is as obscene and unalterable as the stone image which the girls of

Babylon worshipped on certain days. And, greater than nature, also like that image, there is in her, at moments, something abstract and symbolical ; the author raises the ignominy of his conception by a certain sombre hypothesis which makes an impersonal Nana hover over the whole of Paris, and by depriving her of shame as well as conscience, he endows her with the grandeur of natural and fatal forces. When M. Zola succeeds in investing this idea with a concrete form, as in the great picture of the horse-races, when Paris, yelling around Nana, seems to salute in her the queen of lasciviousness, and no longer to be certain whether it acclaims the woman or the horse, that is indeed idealist art and pure poetry.

Do you want examples, at first sight less convincing, but still more significant, of this way of conceiving of and constructing a character ? You will find them in the *Bonheur des Dames* and the *Joie de Vivre*. Notice that these are two ' virtuous ' novels, that is to say, novels in which virtue is depicted and in which it is finally triumphant. But what virtue ? The story of Denise, of that poor and

careful girl who ends by marrying her employer, is the theme for a Sunday-school tale.
Now look at what this Sunday-school tale
becomes. If Nana is vicious in the manner of
an animal, it is also as an animal that Denise
is virtuous, it is thanks to her perfectly
balanced temperament, to her splendid physical health. The author is determined that we
shall not be mistaken about this, that we shall
not accidentally take her for a heroine, nor
believe that she is intentionally careful, and
he comes back to this point I know not how
many times. One could not imagine a more
immodest picture of a virgin. And it is in the
same way that Pauline is good and devoted.
If she has to struggle for a moment, it is
against a physiological influence, and it is not
her will which triumphs, but her health. All
this is quite distinctly stated. Thus, by the
suppression of free will, by the elimination of
the old foundation of classic psychology which
consisted essentially in the struggle between
the will and the passions, M. Zola succeeds in
constructing characters of coarse and imposing
beauty, worn and grandiose images of elementary forces—evil and homicidal like the

plague, or good and beneficent like the sun and like spring.·

Only all approach to subtle psychology disappears. M. Zola's greatest effort does not go beyond painting the unopposed progress of a fixed idea, of a mania or a vice. Either motionless or always dragged along in the same direction, such are his characters. Even when he deals with a very special, very modern case which appears to be essentially psychological, like that of Lazare in the *Joie de Vivre*, he finds some means of applying to it also, in the same spirit, his simplifying methods. He soon effaces the over-subtle shades of feeling or thought, clears away the complexities of mental maladies, and in them also finds the animal beneath the man ! Lazare must doubtless represent a whole section of modern youth, so interesting in its need for rare sensations, its distaste for action, its depravity and enervation of will, its pedantic and perhaps sincere pessimism : now all Lazare's pessimism finally reduces itself to the physical fear of death ; and just as Pauline is as devoted as a little dog, so Lazare's pessimism is that of a cowardly dog.

III

M. Zola employs the same method of audacious simplification in his general compositions. Let us take *Pot-Bouille* as an example, not that it is the best of his novels, but it is one of those in which his manner is most frankly displayed. Exaggerations which by simplifying reality give excessive proportion to some of its characters, are repeated on every ten pages.—There are the domestic servants of the house gossiping from window to window, in the smelling inner courtyard, about the doings of their employers, tearing aside the veils with obscene banter. There is the ironical antithesis between the decent gravity of the great staircase and what takes place behind the fine mahogany doors —this is repeated after every particularly ignoble scene, like the refrain of a ballad. And, just as the house has its great staircase and its mahogany doors, so Uncle Bachelard always has his red nose, Duveyrier his pimples, Madame Josserand her huge breast, Auguste Vabre his left eye drawn by headache ; and little old Josserand has his bands, and old Vabre has his hooks, and Clotilde has her

piano.   M. Zola uses and abuses this device of
'particular signs.'   And everywhere we see
him choosing, abstracting, exaggerating.   If
out of all the magistracy he has been able to
take a Duveyrier (who, moreover, is hardly
more a magistrate than a notary or a pork-
butcher), and out of all the middle-class
women in Paris a Madame Josserand, it is
surely by a selection as bold as that by which
M. Octave Feuillet's women are taken from
the Faubourg Saint-Germain.   Add to this
another application of the same method which
has enabled M. Zola to unite so many contemptible characters in a single house, and to
choose that particular house out of all the
houses in Paris.

Thus conventions abound.   Not a figure
which is not *exaggerated* either in its ignominy
or its dullness ;   their very grouping is an
exceptional fact ;   the least details have been
visibly *chosen* under the empire of a single
tenacious idea, which is to humiliate humanity
and to make it still more ugly with the ugli-
ness of unconscious and base vices.   So true is
this that after a time the falseness of certain
details no longer shocks one, no longer even

appears in the general exaggeration. One has beneath one's eyes the hard and coarse picture, unnaturally large but harmonious and even monotonous, of middle-class squalor, lust, and stupidity ; a picture more than ideal, sibylline and almost apocalyptic in its continuous violence. In it the middle classes are ' the Beast.' The house in the Rue de Choiseul becomes a ' temple ' where infamous mysteries are performed in secret. M. Gourd, the janitor, is its ' beadle.' The Abbé Maudit, melancholy and polished, is its ' master of the ceremonies,' having as his function ' to cover with the mantle of religion the wounds of this decomposed world ' and ' to regulate the proper order of its stupidities and its vices.' At one moment—the caprice of a coarse and mystical imagination—the image of the bleeding Christ rises above this cess-pool. The Vabre building becomes a sort of enormous and symbolical vision. The author ends by lending his own magnifying vision to his characters. The proprietor has let a garret to a pregnant girl, and this woman's belly becomes an obsession to M. Gourd. That belly ' seems to him to throw its shadow over the cold propriety of the courtyard . . . and to fill the building with something shameful which gave an uncomfortable feeling to the walls.' 'At first,' he explains, 'this was hardly visible ; that was possible ; I did not say much about it. I hoped she would show some discretion. Well ! I watched it, it grew visibly larger, it dismayed me by its rapid growth. And look, look, to-day ! She does nothing to reduce it, she gives it full scope. . . . A house like ours made a show of by such a belly ! ' These are unexpected images and grace-notes on the lips of a porter. A strange world in which janitors speak like poets, and all the other people like janitors !

Go through the *Rougon-Macquart* series. You will find in almost all of M. Zola's novels (and certainly in all the latter ones) something similar to that wonderful house in the Rue de Choiseul, some inanimate thing, a forest, a sea, a public-house, or a shop, which serves as the theatre or centre of the drama ; which takes on a superhuman and terrible life ; which personifies some natural or social force superior to individuals, and which at last assumes the aspect of a monstrous Beast, a devourer of souls and a devourer of men. The Beast in *Nana* is Nana herself. In *La Faute de l'Abbé Mouret* the Beast is the park of Paradou, that fantastic forest where everything blooms at the same time, where all odours are mingled, where are assembled all the amorous powers of Cybele, and which, like a divine and irresistible procuress, throws Serge and Albine into one another's arms, and then lulls the little fawness to sleep with its deadly perfumes. In *Le Ventre de Paris* it is the huge size of the Central Markets which causes a copious animal life to flourish about them, and terrifies and submerges the frail and dreamy Florent. In *L'Assommoir* it is old Colombe's public-house with its tin counter and its copper still, like the neck of some mysterious and malevolent animal, that pours over the workmen brutalizing drunkenness, idleness, anger, lust, and unconscious vice. In *Le Bonheur des Dames* it is Mouret's shop, a temple of modern commerce, where the employees deprave and infatuate the women purchasers, a formidable living machine which grinds the smaller shopkeepers in its cog-wheels and devours them. In *La Joie de Vivre* it is the Ocean, at first the

accomplice of Lazare's loves and ambitions,
then his enemy, whose victory completely
ruins the weak head of that disciple o^f
Schopenhauer. M. Zola excels in giving to
things some quiverings, as it were, of that soul
part of which he takes away from men, and,
whilst he gives an almost human life to a
forest, a market-place, a wine-seller's counter,
or a shop, he reduces the sad and base creatures
who move within them to an almost animal
life.

But, whatever that life may be, though it be
incomplete and truncated, he makes them live ;
he has this, the greatest of gifts. And not
only the principal figures, but minor and
subsidiary characters become animate under
the large hands of this modeller of animals.
Doubtless they live at little cost, most often
by virtue of some coarse and energetic special
sign ; but they live, each apart and all together. For he also knows how to animate
groups, how to put masses in movement.
There is in almost all the novels, around the
protagonists, a quantity of secondary characters, a *servum pecus* who often march in a
band, who form the background of the scene ;

but who detach themselves and take part in the dialogue at intervals, like a tragic chorus. There is the chorus of horrible peasants in *La Faute de l'Abbé Mouret* ; the chorus of the friends and relations of Coupeau in *L'Assommoir* ; the chorus of servants in *Pot-Bouille* ; the chorus of employees and that of small shopkeepers in *Le Bonheur des Dames* ; the chorus of fishermen and that of beggars in *La Joie de Vivre*. Through these the leading figures are mingled with a large portion of humanity ; and since this humanity, as we have seen, is itself mingled with the life of things, there emerges from these vast combinations an impression of life, almost uniquely bestial and material, but swarming with living beings, profound, vast and unlimited.

IV

This impression is a sad one, and M. Zola wishes it thus. Never perhaps has a pessimistic determination been carried to such excesses. And the evil has only gone on increasing since his first novels. At least in the early stages of this miry epic poem, one still saw something like the intoxication of

antique naturalism (exasperated, it is true,
by the Christian notion of sin and by modern
' nervousness '). In the exuberant pastoral
of Miette and Silvère (*La Fortune des Rougon*)
in the Paradisaical nuptials of the Abbé
Mouret and Albine, even in the bestial idyll of
Cadine and Majolin among the heaps of beans
in the markets, M. Zola appeared at least to
glorify physical love and its works. But he
now seems to have a hatred and terror of all
this flesh by which he is obsessed. He seeks
to humiliate it ; he lingers in the lower depths
of human nature, amid all that is most insult-
ing to human pride in the play of the forces of
blood and nerves. He digs out and displays
the secret deformities of the flesh and its secret
vileness. He multiplies around adultery the
circumstances that degrade it, that make it
vulgar and disgusting (*Une Page d'Amour* and
Pot-Bouille). He spurns love, reduces it to a
tyrannical need and a squalid function (*Pot-
Bouille*). The greater part of his novels is an
impassioned commentary on the words *surgit
amari aliquid*. Of woman he sees no more
than the defiling mysteries of her sex (*Pot-
Bouille* and *La Joie de Vivre*). With the

sombre ardour of a fakir, he curses life at its
source and man in his mother's womb. In
man he sees the brute, in love copulation, in
maternity obstetrics. Slowly and sadly he
stirs up the secretions, the humours, all that is
kept hidden in physical humanity. What a
horrible and lamentable picture is that of the
way 'that slut Adèle' spends her nights !
And what a pathological drama, how like the
dream of some embittered medical student, is
the atrocious confinement of Louise in *La Joie
de Vivre !*

And neither clinical horrors nor moral
putrefaction are enough for him, although
there is a complete collection of them, going
from the loves of Maxime to those of Léon
Josserand, and passing through the fantasies
of Baptiste, of Satin, of the little Angèle, and
of the thin Lisa. He must have curious
physiological states such as the case of
Théophile Vabre or that of Madame Campar-
don. The mine is inexhaustible, and if he
must now combine corporal infirmities with
lusts and follies, the story of the Rougon-
Macquarts will yet have fine chapters in it.

Thus bestiality and imbecility are in M.

Zola's eyes man's very essence. His work presents to us so prodigious a mass of beings who are either idiots or a prey to the 'sixth sense,' that there exhales from it—like a miasma or the reek from a dung-heap—for most readers a feeling of profound disgust, for others one of black and heavy sadness. How shall we explain this strange determination of the author of *Pot-Bouille* ? Shall we say that he likes force above all things, and that nothing is stronger than that which is blind, nothing is stronger than the instincts of animalism, nor than exhaustion and impotence (thus he has far more brutes than scoundrels), and nothing is more invariable, more formidable by its eternity, its universality, and its unconsciousness than stupidity? Or rather, does not M. Zola, in truth, see the world as he paints it ? Yes, there is in him the pessimism of a tempted ascetic, and, before the flesh and its adventures, a morose intoxication which invades his whole being, and which he could not shake off even if he would. If it is true that the men of the present day reproduce, with more complication, the types of past ages, M. Zola has been, in the early

Middle Ages, a very chaste and very serious monk, but with too healthy and too vigorous an imagination, who saw the devil in everything, and who cursed the corruption of his time in obscene and hyperbolical language.

It is therefore a great injustice to accuse M. Zola of immorality, or to believe that he speculates on the bad instincts of readers. In the midst of low obscenities, among visions of places of ill-fame or of clinical studies, he remains grave. If he accumulates certain details, be sure that with him it is a matter of conscience. As he claims to paint reality, and as he is persuaded that it is ignoble, he shows it to us thus, with the scruples of a soul which is delicate in its own way, which does not want to deceive us, and which gives us good measure. Sometimes he forgets himself, he brushes in vast pictures from which the ignominy of the flesh is absent ; but suddenly a remorse seizes him ; he remembers that the Beast is everywhere, and, in order not to fail in his duty, at the moment when this is least expected he slips in a lewd detail and as it were a *memento* of the universal filth. These species of *repentances* are especially remarkable in the development of the characters of Denise and Pauline (*Au Bonheur des Dames* and *La Joie de Vivre*). And, as I have said, a frightful melancholy exhales from all this physiological movement.

V

If the impression is sad, it is powerful. I compliment those subtle and delicate spirits for whom measure, decency, and correction are so essentially all a writer requires, that, even after *La Conquête de Plassans, La Faute de l'Abbé Mouret, L'Assommoir,* and *La Joie de Vivre,* they hold M. Zola in slight literary esteem, and tell him to go back to school because his classical studies have not been thorough, and perhaps he does not always write perfectly well. I could not rise to so distinguished a judgment. If one refuses everything else to M. Zola, is it possible to deny him creative power, restricted if you will, but prodigious in the domain in which it is exercised? Struggle against it as I may, even those brutalities impress me, I do not know how, by their number, and those obscenities by their mass. With the regular efforts of a grime-stained Hercules, M. Zola arranges in heaps the dung of the Augean stables (it has even been said that he has added to it). One is amazed and alarmed by its size, and by the labour that has been needed to make so fine a heap. One of M. Zola's virtues is indefatigable and patient vigour. He has an excellent vision of concrete things, of all the external side of life, and he possesses a special faculty for representing what he sees—the power of retaining and accumulating greater quantity of details than any other describer of the same school, and of doing this coldly and calmly, without lassitude or disgust, and of giving to all things the same clear and crude prominence. So that the unity of each picture no longer consists, as is the case with the classics, in the subordination of details (which in their case were not numerous) to the whole, but, if I may so express myself, in their interminable monochrome. Yes, this artist has a marvellous power of piling things up so as to produce a single effect. I am quite ready to believe what is told of him, that he always writes at the same rate and fills the same number of pages every day. He con-

structs a book as a mason builds a wall, by
putting unhewn stones one on top of the other,
without hurrying, indefinitely. That is certainly fine in its own way, and it is perhaps
one of the forms of that prolonged patience of
which Buffon speaks, which is genius. This
gift, joined to the others, at all events, gives
him a robust originality.

Nevertheless, many people persist in refus-
ing him the quality which, it is said, preserves
works—style. But here it is first of all
necessary to distinguish between his critical or
polemical works and his novels. The books in
which he had to give expression to abstract
ideas are, in truth, not always well written,
whether it be that the embarrassment and
ambiguity of thought communicate themselves to the style, or that M. Zola is naturally
incapable of rendering ideas with complete
exactness. The form of his novels is much
more defensible. But even in these it is
necessary to distinguish. M. Zola has never
been an impeccable writer nor very sure with
his pen ; but in his early novels (up to *Nana*,
it seems to me) he took more trouble with his
writing ; his style was more wrought and

richer. There are, even if we consider nothing but the form, some truly fine pages, of great brilliancy and quite pure enough, in *La Fortune des Rougon* and in *La Faute de l'Abbé Mouret*. Since *Nana*, at the same time as under the pretext of truth he more and more forgets decency, one can say that under colour of simplicity and out of hatred of romanticism (which is at once his father and his pet aversion) he has set himself to despise style a little, to write much more quickly, in a manner that is ' more fine and large,' without bothering much about the details of his phrasing. In both of these two manners, but especially in the second, it is not difficult to find faults that are offensive enough and that are particularly cruel to those who are accustomed to converse with the classics, to those who have had a good university education, to old professors who know their own speech well — improprieties of language, strange incongruities, a surprising mixture of far-fetched expressions, ' poetic ' expressions as they used to be called, and low or trivial phrases, certain bad habits of style, sometimes inaccuracies, and above all, a continual

straining ; never any of the more delicate
shades or any refinement. Yes, all this is
true, and I am very sorry for it. But, in the
first place, it is not true everywhere, far from
it. And then as everything in the novels is
constructed on a large scale, intended to be
comprehended at once and without close
examination, we must not cavil over phrases,
but take them as they have been written, in
blocks and in large sections, and judge the
worth of the style by the total effect of the
picture. You will admit that, upon the
whole, such a heap of phrases, though all of
them are not irreproachable, yet end by giving
us a vast and impressive vision of the objects,
and that this magnifying style, without any of
the finer shades, and sometimes without precision, is eminently suitable, by its monotonous exaggerations and its multiplied insist-
ences, for rendering with grandeur the great
and general effect of concrete things.

VI

Germinal, the last novel that has appeared,
marvellously confirms the description of M.
Zola's work which I have attempted. Every-

thing which I thought I saw in the former novels abounds in *Germinal*, and one can say that never have either M. Zola's moroseness and his epic faculty, or the methods which they imply and whose use they demand, been more powerfully employed than in that imposing and sombre book.

The subject is very simple—it is the story of a strike, or rather it is the poem of *the* strike. Some miners, as a result of a measure that seems to them to be unjust, refuse to go down into the pits. Hunger exasperates them to pillage and murder. Order is restored by the troops. On the day that the workers go down again, the mine is flooded and some of the leading characters are drowned. This last catastrophe, the deed of an anarchist workman, is the only feature which distinguishes this strike from so many others.

It is thus the story, not of a man or of some men, but of a multitude. I do not know any novel in which such masses are made to live and move, at one moment it crawls and swarms, at another it is carried along in a dizzy movement by the urge of blind instincts. The poet, with his robust patience, with his gloomy brutality, with his power of evocation, unrolls a series ·of vast and lamentable pictures, composed of monochrome details which pile up, pile up, ascend and spread out like a tide—a day in the mine, a day in the workmen's dwellings, a meeting of the strikers in a clearing of the woods, the furious rush of three thousand unhappy souls over the flat country, the impact of this mass against the soldiers, ten days of lingering death in the flooded mine. . . .

M. Zola has given a magnificent rendering of all that is fatal, blind, impersonal, irresistible in a drama of this sort, the contagion of assembled anger, the violent and easily enraged collective soul of the crowd.   He often collects the scattered heads into one formidable mass, and this is the sort of breath he pours forth :

' The women appeared, nearly a thousand women, with dishevelled hair, loosened by the journey, in rags showing their bare skin, the nakedness of women weary of giving birth to starvelings. Some of them held their little one in their arms, lifting it up and moving it like a flag of mourning and of vengeance. Others, younger, with the inflated throats of female warriors, brandished sticks, while the old women howled so loudly that the tendons of their fleshless necks seemed to break. And the men sprung out afterwards, two thousand furious men, haulers, hewers, menders, a compact mass which advanced in a single block, crowded together and so mixed up that one could not see either their faded breeches or their tattered woollen vests which were effaced in the same dirty uniformity. Their eyes burned ; one only saw the holes of dark mouths singing the *Marseillaise*, the verses of which were lost in confused bellowings accompanied by the rattle of clogs on the hard ground. Above their heads, amid bristling bars of iron, an axe was carried along, borne upright, and this single axe, which was as it were the standard of the band, looked in the clear sky like the profile of the blade of a guillotine.

' Anger, hunger, those two months of

suffering, and this wild, helter-skelter rush over the fields had lengthened the placid faces of the Montsou colliers into the jaws of wild beasts. At this moment the sun was setting ; its last rays, of a sombre purple, stained the plain with the colour of blood. Then the journey seemed to be a drift of blood ; the women and men continued to run on, bleeding like butchers in a slaughter-yard.'

However, the drama had to be concentrated on some individuals. Accordingly, the poet has shown us, on the side of the workers, the Maheu family and their ' lodger,' Étienne, and on the side of the Company, the Hennebeau family, and about forty secondary figures in both camps ; but always there is the swarming and growling multitude around those figures. Étienne himself, the leader of the strike, is himself dragged onward more than he drags on others.

The heads which emerge for a moment and which can be distinguished from the crowd are those of Maheu, a worthy fellow, a thoughtful, resigned, and reasonable man who little by little becomes a fanatic ; the woman

Maheus, with Estelle, her latest born, *always* hanging at her pale breast, the woman whose man and whose children are killed by hunger, by the soldiers' guns, and by the mine, and who appears at the end like a *Mater Dolorosa*, a stupid and terrible Niobe ; Catherine, who plays the part of young girl in this dark epic, always wearing the trousers of a labourer, who has the sort of beauty, modesty, and charm that she can have ; Chaval, the traitor, who is *always* ' mouthing ' ; Étienne, the Socialist workman, of rather more refined a nature than his companions, with his sudden outbursts of anger, and the alcoholism which he has inherited from Gervaise Coupeau ; Alzire, the little hunchback, so gentle, and *always* acting the part of a little woman ; old Mouque, who only speaks once, and old Bonnemort, who is *always* spitting out tobacco juice, Rasseneur, the old workman who has become a publican, a fat, unctuous, and prudent revolutionist ; Pluchart, the itinerant Socialist lecturer, *always* hoarse and hurried ; Maigrat, the grocer, a sort of Pasha who pays himself out of the miners' wives and daughters ; Mouquette, the good girl, and simple-minded

prostitute ; the sly Pierronne, who has the
regular characteristics of a prostitute ; Jeanlin,
the wretched marauder with his broken paws
and freckles, his projecting ears and his green
eyes, who treacherously kills a young soldier,
for nothing, instinctively, and for the sake of
pleasure ; Lydie and Bébert, *always* terrorized
by Jeanlin ; Brulé, the old woman whose
husband has been killed by the mine, *always*
moaning and shaking her witch-like arms ;
Hennebeau, the manager, a cold and exact
official, with a wound in his heart, a husband
tormented by a Messalina who refuses herself
to nobody but him ; Négrel, the brown little
engineer, brave and sceptical and his aunt's
lover ; Deneulin, the energetic and adventurous man of business ; the Grégoires, comfortable and easy shareholders, and Cécile, and
Jeanne, and Lucie, and Levaque, and Boute-
loup, and old Quandieu, and Jules, the little
soldier ; and the old horse, Bataille, ' fat and
shining with an air of good-nature,' and the
young horse, Trompette, haunted in the depth
of the mine by a vision of meadows and sunshine (for M. Zola loves animals and endows
them with at least as much soul as men—

remember the dog, Mathieu, and the cat, Minouche, in *La Joie de Vivre*) ; and apart from all this world, the Russian Souvarine, fair and with a girl's features, *always* silent, contemptuous, and gentle—all figures strongly marked by a ' particular sign ' the mention of which returns regularly, who stand upright and come to life in some way that I do not know, almost by the sole virtue of that repeated sign.

Their life is above all an external life ; but the drama which M. Zola has conceived does not require more psychology than he can give to it. The soul of such a mass consists of very simple instincts. The inferior beings who hold a subordinate position in the book, are moved, as they ought to be, by physical necessities, and by very crude ideas which become *images*, and which at length fascinate them and make them act. ' All misfortune disappeared as if driven away by a great flash of sunlight, and, as if by fairy enchantment, justice descended from Heaven. . . . A new society sprang up as in dreams in a day, an immense city as splendid as a mirage, in which each citizen lived by his own toil and took his

share in the common joys.' The inner life
even of Étienne ought to be reduced to a very
simple matter, for he is hardly superior to his
companions—aspirations towards absolute
justice, confused ideas as to the means of
achieving it ; sometimes the pride of thinking
more than the rest, and sometimes an almost
avowed feeling of his own incapacity ; the
pedantry of the workman who has read, and
the discouragement that follows enthusiasm ;
middle-class tastes and intellectual feelings
mingling with his apostle's fervour. This is
all, and it is enough. As for Souvarine, it is
with deliberate intention that M. Zola leaves
him enigmatical, and only shows us the
external side of him—his anarchism is only
there in order to form a striking contrast with
the uncertain and sentimental Socialism of the
French workman, and in order to prepare for
the final catastrophe. It is said, perhaps
with truth, that M. Zola does not possess to a
high degree the gift of entering into souls, of
analysing them, of noting the origin and progress of ideas and feelings within them, or
the way in which they echo a thousand
external influences : so he has here desired not

to write the story of a soul, but that of a crowd.

And it is not a drama of feelings either, that he has wished to write, but a drama of sensations, an entirely material drama. The feelings are reduced to instincts or something close to them, and the sufferings are especially physical sufferings, as when Jeanlin has his legs broken, when little Alzire dies of hunger, when Catherine climbs two thousand feet of stairs, or when she dies in the pit in Étienne's arms, close by Chaval's corpse. It will be said that it is easy to stir the heart or to jangle the nerves at such a cost, and that this is the crudest melodrama. Do you think so ? But these deaths and these tortures are drama itself, for M. Zola had no intention of composing a psychological tragedy. And there is more than the description of atrocious spectacles ; there are the novelist's gloomy pity and compassion which a determination based on the philosophy of pessimism turns into an impassibility that is cruel for us as well as for him. He is not one of those to whom moral pain is nobler than physical suffering. In what is it more noble, since our feelings are as involuntary as our sensations ? And then, let us be sincere, and is it not the suffering of the body that is the most terrible ? And is it not above all this suffering that makes the world so miserable ?

And for those holocausts of flesh there are the executioner and the god, both of them ' Beasts.' The executioner is the mine, the beast that devours men. The god is that mysterious being to whom the mine belongs and who grows fat on the hunger of the miners ; he is a monstrous and invisible idol, crouching somewhere, one knows not where, like the God Mithra in his sanctuary. And the two beasts are regularly evoked in turn, the beast that kills, and the other, the beast that causes her to kill. And at intervals we hear the ' heavy and long respiration ' of the beast that kills (it is the noise of the exhaust pump). She lives, she is so much alive that at last she dies :

> ' And then a frightful thing was seen ; one saw the machine, dismembered in its whole body, its limbs torn to pieces, struggling against death. It moved, it stretched out its connecting-rod, its

giant's knee, as if to stand up ; but it expired, broken and engulfed. Its chimney alone, ninety feet high, remained upright though shaken, like a mast in a hurricane. One thought that it was going to crumble and fly into dust, when suddenly it subsided in a single block, swallowed up by the earth, melted like a colossal candle, and nothing remained on top, not even the point of the lightning-conductor. It was ended ; the evil beast, crouching in those hollows, gorged with human flesh, no longer drew her long and heavy breath. The entire Voreux had just fallen into the pit.'

And how many other symbolical evocations there are ! The bloody rag torn away by the women from Maigrat, is also an evil beast that is finally crushed and trampled and spat upon. Old Bonnemort, idiotic, deformed, and hideous, strangling the plump, fair, and gentle Cécile Grégoire, is ancient and irresponsible Hunger hurling herself with fatal spring upon irresponsible Idleness. And every moment, by methods that are frankly and ingenuously displayed, but that hold us nevertheless, the poet, in a sinister manner, mingles nature with his pictures in order to heighten them and make them the more horrible. The miners' meeting is held before a background of pale moonlight, and the journey of the three thousand desperate men and women is performed in the blood-stained light of the setting sun. And it is with a symbol that the book ends. Étienne leaves the mine on a spring morning, one of those mornings when the ' buds are bursting into green leaves ' and when the fields are ' trembling with the growth of the grass.' At the same time he hears deep blows underneath his feet, the blows of his comrades tapping in the mine : ' Still, still, more and more distinctly, as if they were drawing closer to the soil, his comrades kept on tapping. Under the kindled stars, on this morning of youth, it was with this murmur that the countryside was big. Men were growing ; a black, avenging army was sprouting in the furrows, growing for the harvest of a future age whose germination was soon to burst through the earth.' And hence the title of the book.

What does this enigmatic end mean ?

What is this future revolution ? Is it the pacific accession of the disinherited or the destruction of the old world ? Is it the reign of justice or .the long-delayed feast of the greatest number ? This is mystery, or is it merely rhetoric ? For the rest of the novel does not contain an atom of hope or of illusion. I recognize, moreover, M. Zola's lofty impartiality. The great exploiters are not seen and do not see. We only perceive the Grégoires, small shareholders, worthy people whose daughter is killed by the exploited. And as for Hennebeau, the manager, he is as much to be pitied as the starving workmen. ' Beneath the window groans burst forth with redoubled violence : " Bread ! Bread ! Bread ! "—" You fools," said M. Hennebeau from between his clenched teeth ; " am I happy ? " '

Suffering and despair from top to bottom ! But at least these wretches have the animal Venus to console them. They ' love ' like dogs, pell-mell, everywhere, at every hour. There is a chapter in which one cannot take a single step without walking upon couples. And this is astonishing enough in the case of dull-blooded men, broken down by toil, in a cold and rainy district. They ' love ' in the depths of the flooded mine, and it is after six days of agony in it that Étienne becomes Catherine's lover. And I would prefer that he had not become her lover, the instinctive modesty which they felt in one another's presence being almost the sole vestige of higher humanity which the writer has allowed to exist in his bestial poem.

Here and there in this epic of pain, hunger, lust, and death, there breaks forth the lamentation of Hennebeau, which gives the moral of the story and obviously expresses M. Zola's thought. ' A terrible bitterness poisoned his mouth . . . *the uselessness of everything, the eternal pain of existence.*'

' Who was the fool who said that the happiness of this world lay in the division of wealth ? If those revolutionary visionaries could demolish society and build up another, they would not add a joy to humanity, they would not take away a pain from it, by each of them cutting off his own slice of cake. They would even extend the earth's misery, they would one day make the very dogs howl with despair, when they had left the tranquil satisfaction of the instincts and risen to the unsatiated suffering of the passions. No, the only good was not to exist, and if one did exist, to be a tree, to be a stone, to be still less, to be the grain of sand which did not bleed under the heel of those who passed over it.'

A band of wretches, roused by hunger and instinct, attracted by a crude dream, moved by fatal forces, and advancing in whirls and eddies to break themselves against a superior force—that is the drama. Men appearing like waves on a sea of darkness and unconsciousness—that is the very simple philosophical vision into which the drama resolves itself. M. Zola leaves it to the psychologists to write the monograph of each of those waves and to make of them a centre, and as it were a microcosm. He has only an imagination for vast material wholes, and infinite external details. But I ask myself whether anybody has ever had this in the same degree.

VII

I repeat in conclusion, and with greater confidence after having read *Germinal*, was I not right to call M. Zola an epic poet? And are not the dominant characters in these long narratives precisely those of epic poetry? With a little good-will, and by straining words a little, one could maintain and carry further this comparison, and there would be a great basis of truth beneath the artifice of this rhetorical game.

The subject of the epic is a national subject, interesting to a whole people, intelligible to a whole race. The subjects chosen by M. Zola are always very general, can be understood by everybody, have nothing special, exceptional, ' curious '—the story of a family of workmen who sink into drunkenness, of a courtesan who fascinates and ruins men, of a prudent girl who ends by marrying her employer, a strike of miners, etc., and all these narratives together have at least the pretension of forming the typical history of a single family. The *Rougon-Macquart* history is thus, as in an epic poem, the collective history of an epoch.

The characters in epic poetry are not less general than the subject, and, as they represent vast groups, they appear to be larger than in nature. It is the same with M. Zola's characters, although this is reached by a contrary method. Whilst the old poets endeavour to deify their figures, we have seen that he animalizes his. But this even adds to the epic appearance ; for he manages, through the falsehood of this reduction, to give to modern figures the simplicity of primitive types. He sets masses in motion, as in epic poetry. And the *Rougon-Macquart* series has also its marvels. In epic poetry the gods were originally the personifications of natural forces. M. Zola lends to those forces, either freely let loose or disciplined by human industry, a terrifying life, the beginnings of a soul, an obscure and monstrous will. The marvels in the *Rougon-Macquart* series are Paradou, old Colombe's dram-shop, Octave Mouret's shop, the mine in *Germinal*.

There is an artless and rudimentary philosophy in epic poetry. It is the same with the *Rougon-Macquart* series. The only difference is that the wisdom of the old poets is generally optimistic, and consoles and ennobles man as much as it can, whilst that of M. Zola is black and desperate.   But in both there is the same simplicity, the same artlessness of conception. Finally and especially, the procedure of M. Zola's novels is, I know not how, that of the ancient epics, by the slow power, the broad sweep, the tranquil accumulation of details, the absolute frankness of the narrator's methods.   He no more hurries than Homer does.   He is as much interested (in another spirit) in Gervaise's kitchen as the old singer is in that of Achilles.   He is not afraid of repetitions ;   the same phrases return in the same words, and from time to time we hear the ' snoring ' of the shop in *Le Bonheur des Dames*, the ' heavy and prolonged breathing ' of the machine in *Germinal* as in the *Iliad* we hear the moaning of the sea, πολυφλοςβοῖο θαλάσσης.

If then we gather up all that we have said, it will not appear too absurd to define the *Rougon-Macquart* series as a pessimist epic of human animalism.

GUY DE MAUPASSANT

OUGHT I, before speaking of M. Guy de Maupassant, to excuse myself to the reader, who is doubtless a respectable person, ought I to surround myself with oratorical precautions, to affirm that I do not approve of the deeds and gestures of Madame Bonderoi or M. Tourneveau, nor of the visible indulgence of the narrator towards them, and ought I only to insinuate that he has some talent while I make severe and express reserves as to the nature of the subjects he prefers and the amusement which he procures us—well, in spite of ourselves? Or should I take the air as Théophile Gautier did in a famous preface, of flouting middle-class modesty with its musty virtues and its moth-eaten chastities, declaring that respectable people are always ugly and that, besides, they commit horrors in secret, proclaiming the artist's right to indecency, and seriously affirming that art purifies everything ? I shall do neither. It is not my business to reprimand M. Guy de Maupassant who writes as he likes. I only regret on his account that his work has brought him a somewhat mixed crowd of admirers, and that many dullards appreciate him for something quite different from his great talent. It is cruel to see an old Philistine on the look-out for certain truffles not making any difference between those of M. de Maupassant and the others. And that is why I deplore the fact that he is not always decent. But, moreover, if his tales were solely remarkable for their author's impudence, I should not speak of them ; and it need not be said that, wishing to re-read them here in good company and to make some remarks about them, I shall pass quickly over what needs to be passed over.

Let us concern ourselves only with his tales—that is to say, with the most considerable part of his work, with that in which he is absolutely without an equal.

I

The tale is with us a national literary form. Under the name of ' fabliau ' and then of

' nouvelle,' it is almost as old as our literature.
It is one of·the tastes of the race, which likes
narratives, but which is alert and light, and
which, if it tolerates long ones, sometimes
prefers them short, and if it likes them to be
pathetic, does not despise them if they are
merry.   The tale has thus been contemporary
with the *chansons de geste*, and it existed before
prose romance.

Naturally, it has not been the same in all
epochs.   Very varied in the Middle Ages, by
turns broad, religious, moral, or marvellous,
it was particularly broad in the sixteenth
and seventeenth centuries.   In the following
century, ' philosophy ' and ' sensibility ' make
their entry into it, and also a deeper and more
refined libertinage.

In these latter years the tale, for a long time
neglected, has had a sort of revival.   We are
more and more hurried ; our minds require
rapid pleasures or emotions in brief shocks :
we require our novels to be condensed if
possible, or abridged if there is nothing better
to offer us.   The newspapers having felt this,
hit upon a plan of printing short stories by
way of leading articles, and the public judged

that, tale for tale, these latter were the more
entertaining. There thus arose a Pleiad of
story-tellers : first, Alphonse Daudet and
Paul Arène, and, in a special class, the writers
for *La Vie Parisienne*—Ludovic Halévy, Gyp,
Richard O'Monroy—and those for the *Figaro*
and *Gil Blas*—Coppée, Théodore de Banville,
Armand Silvestre, Catulle Mendes, Guy de
Maupassant, each of them having his own
manner, and some a very pretty manner.

These little narratives of our contemporaries
do not entirely resemble, as is thought, those
of the story-tellers of our older literature, of
Bonaventure Despériers, of La Fontaine, of
Grécourt, or of Piron. You know what is the
habitual theme of those patriarchs, the almost unique subject of their pleasantries.
And these matters always make people laugh,
and even the gravest persons do not resist
them. Why is this ? One understands that
certain images may be agreeable, for man is
weak ; but why do they make people laugh ?
Why do the coarser sides of the comedy of
love make almost everybody mirthful ? The
reason is that, in truth, it is a comedy ; that
there is an ironical and diverting contrast

between the tone, the sentiments of love, and what is easily grotesque in its rites. And it is a comedy also that is given us by the eternal and invincible revolt of the instinct in question, in a society duly regulated and schooled, swathed in laws, traditions, and preservative beliefs—that revolt bursting forth readily at the most unexpected moments, from beneath the most respectable garb, suddenly belying the most assured dignity or the most secure ingenuity, and baffling the strongest authority or the most careful precautions. And perhaps also the jolly tricks played by our inferior nature on social conventions flatter the instinct of rebellion and the liking for free life that every man brings with him when he comes into the world. It is therefore inevitable that these things should make people laugh, even if one wished to be over-particular and delicate, and there is truly some philosophy in the easy gaiety of our fathers.

This old and inexhaustible spring is to be found in our story-tellers of to-day, above all in three or four whom I need not name. But it is curious to seek for what is added to it, particularly in M. de Maupassant. He seems to

158

me to have the temperament of our story-
tellers of former days, and I would imagine
that under Francis I. he would have written
tales like Bonaventure Despériers, and under
Louis XIV. like Jean de La Fontaine. Let us
see, then, what it is that he derives from his
own age, from the literature that surrounds
him, and after that we shall say why and
wherefore we nevertheless regard him as a
classic in his own department.

II

I believe that one can say, without making
too great a mistake, that M. de Maupassant's
tales are almost for us what those of La Fontaine were for his contemporaries. A comparison between the two collections may
therefore suggest instructive reflections on
the differences of times and of story-tellers.

We read La Fontaine's tales on the desks
of our schoolrooms, with a Virgil close at hand
to cover up the prohibited volume at the
slightest movement of the usher. The scape-
graces of the Moronval Institution read them
even in chapel during the short mass on Sun-
days, and boast of it. At least they believe

they read them, but they search them for
only one thing. After schooldays, we devour
contemporary literature, and if we chanced to
find again in our hands the little narratives
that charmed Henrietta of England, we should
find them insipid. But later, when we have
read everything and are, if not surfeited, at
least satiated ; when we are able to detach
ourselves from the things we read, to enjoy
them as an amusement that only interests
and moves the intelligence, La Fontaine's
tales, seen in their proper light and in the
style of a somewhat distant spectacle, can be
very diverting. That joyous world, almost
quite artificial, pleases us for this very reason.
Seven or eight figures, always the same, as in
the Italian comedy : the monk or the parish
priest, the mule-driver or the peasant, the
worthy husband, who is a merchant or a
judge at Florence, the stripling, the nun, the
simpleton, the serving-maid, and the mistress, each having his or her part to play and
his or her physiognomy, and never acting
but in strict accordance with his character ;
all, except a few husbands, satisfied with life,
cheerful and pawky, and all, from the large

red face to the pretty face framed in a veil, occupied with one single thing in the world, one thing alone ; for the stage, a convent, a garden, the room of an inn, or a vague palace in Italy ; abominable tricks, disguises, substitutions, blunders, slight plots founded on improbable hazards and credulities ; an extreme simplicity, a delicious good-nature in all this fantasy, and here and there a bit of reality, very lifelike touches, but scattered and put in as they come ; sometimes also an expressive little bit of landscape, a little thread of true tenderness, and a little shade of melancholy— these, taken as a whole, make up La Fontaine's tales. The artifice and the uniformity of the characters does not prevent these trifles from being charming from their dexterity, from their incommunicable grace ; but one immediately foresees in what the tales of to-day are going to differ from those of two centuries ago.

I should like to find a tale by La Fontaine and a short story by M. de Maupassant of which the themes were almost similar, so that the mere comparison of the two narratives would throw light for us on the object of our search. But I can discover none, precisely because M. de Maupassant takes his subjects and his details from close and living reality. Unless one is able to see, by making a great effort, some resemblance between, say, *Clochette* and *Une Partie de Campagne*, for here and there we find the eternal ' oaristys ' and a lad taking a lass into the woods in spring. La Fontaine's tale is fifty lines in length ; it is delicious and, as it happens, truly poetical, light, and exquisite. You remember the youth

' Qui dans les prés, sur le bord d'un ruisseau,
  Vous cajolait la jeune bachelette
  Aux blanches dents, aux pieds nus, au corps gent,
  Pendant qu'Io, portant une clochette,
  Aux environs allait l'herbe mangeant . . .' [1]

and then the said young ' bachelor ' turning away ' in the quiet of the night ' a heifer whose bell he had muted, and the last verse, with its prolonged, indefinite charm :

　　　　　　' O belles, evitez
　　Le fond des bois et leur vaste silence,' [2]

---

[1] ' Who in the meadows, by the bank of a stream, was coaxing the young lass with white teeth, bare feet, and well-moulded body, whilst Io, carrying a bell, went about eating the grass all round.'

[2] ' O fair ones, avoid the depths of the wood and their vast silence.'

Now see how in *Une Partie de Campagne*
everything is precise and ' realistic ' : do
you remember Monsieur and Madame Dufour,
their daughter, Henriette, on a swing at the
Bezons inn, and the two boatmen, and the
little wood of L'Ile-aux-Anglais, and the
mother's walk forming a counterpart to the
daughter's, and, in the background, M. Dufour
and the yellow-haired young man, Henriette's
husband that is to be, all this giving the idyll
a savour of ironical reality by turns sad and
grotesque. Notice that La Fontaine's heroine is a lass ' with well-moulded body,' and
that M. de Maupassant's a tall dark girl.
This difference appears slight enough : it is,
however, big with consequences ; it implies
two diverse views of poetry.

Similarly, we can ask ourselves what would
the *Courtisane Amoureuse* become from M. de
Maupassant's pen. The tale is very pretty,
truly tender and touching ; but it happens
one knows not where—in Italy, I think.
The ' environment ' is of no account, the
characters have no individual features. (Do
not take this for a criticism, it is only an
observation.) It is evident that if M. de

Maupassant encountered this subject, he would have treated it in quite a different way. Constance, I suppose, would no longer be the graceful and only half-real creature of the Italian tale ; she would be a ' girl ' and would have some special characteristic. The hero would be a student, or a young artist, or a shopman. The story would begin, I imagine, at the Bullier and would culminate somewhere else no less real, and there would be much fruit of observation, and, besides the action, many significant, moving, picturesque, or cruel details. But, by the way, I remember : What are the first thirty pages of *Sapho* but the *Courtisane Amoureuse* accommodated to the taste of the present day ?

What pleases us, then, is no longer quite what pleased our fathers. In the first place, the tale, in M. de Maupassant's hands, has become realistic. Glance through its themes. You will see in almost all of them some little fact seized in passing, interesting for some reason or other, as evidence of stupidity, unthinkingness, egoism, sometimes even of human goodness, or pleasing by some unexpected contrast, some irony of things, at all events something that has *happened*, or at least an observation made from life, which little by little has assumed in the writer's mind the living form of a short story.

And then, instead of the mule-drivers, gardeners, and lovers of the old tales, instead of Mazet and old Pierre, we have peasants of both sexes like Gaffer Vallin and his servant Rose, Gaffer Omont, Gaffer Hauchecorne, Gaffer Chicot, and Mother Magloire, and how many others !

Instead of worthy merchants and lawyers similar in their fates and their faces, here is M. Dufour, ironmonger ; M. Caravan, chief clerk at the Admiralty ; Morin, haberdasher. Instead of the joyous gossips and the artful nuns, here is little Madame Lelievre, Marroca, Rachel and Francesca Rondoli. And I shall not say by what convents M. de Maupassant replaces those of La Fontaine.

One consequence of this realism is that these tales are not always gay. Some of them are sad, and some are extremely brutal. This was inevitable. Most of the subjects are taken from classes and ' environments ' in which instincts are stronger and blinder.

Hence it is hardly possible for one to be always laughing. Almost all the characters become ugly or gloomy merely in passing from the artificial atmosphere of the old tales into the crude light of the real world. What a difference, for example, between the ' lass,' the gay girl conceived in a general fashion, in the air, as an amiable and lively creature

' Qui fait plaisir aux enfants sans souci,' [1]

and the courtesan as she is, in all the truth of her condition, of her behaviour, of her language, classed and, more than classed, inscribed ! It is not at all the same personage, not at all. And so for the rest.

Add to this that in spite of his natural gaiety, M. de Maupassant, like many writers of his generation, affects a moroseness, a misanthropy that gives an excessively bitter flavour to several of his narratives. It is evident that he likes and searches for the most violent manifestations of love reduced to desire, of egoism, of brutality, of simple ferocity. To speak only of his peasants, some of them eat black-puddings over their grand-

[1] ' Who gives pleasure to children without a care.'

father's corpse which they have stuffed into
the trough so that they may be able to sleep
in their only bed.   Another, an innkeeper, who
has an interest in the death of an old woman,
rids himself of her gaily by killing her with
brandy in every way he could.   Another, a
worthy fellow, rapes his servant, then, having
married her, beats her to a jelly because she
does not give him children.   Others, these
latter outside the law, poachers and loafers
of the Seine, amuse themselves royally by
shooting an old donkey with a gun loaded
with salt ; and I also commend to you the
amusements of Saint Antony with his Prus-
sian.

M. de Maupassant searches out with no
less predilection the most ironical conjunctions of ideas or of facts, the most unexpected
and most shocking combinations of feelings,
those most likely to wound in us some illusion or some moral delicacy.   The comic and
the sensual mingling in these almost sacrileg-
ious combinations, not precisely to purify them,
but to prevent them from being painful.
While others depict for us war and its effects
on the fields of battle or in families, M. de

Maupassant, hewing out for himself from this common material a portion that is indeed his own, shows us the effects of the invasion in a special world and even in houses which we usually designate by euphemisms. You remember Boule-de-Suif's astonishing sacrifice, and the unheard-of conduct of those whom she obliged, and, in *Mademoiselle Fifi*, Rachel's revolt, the stab, the girl in the steeple who is afterwards brought back and embraced by the parish priest and at last married by a patriot who has no prejudices. Remark that Rachel and Boule-de-Suif are certainly, along with Miss Harriet, little Simon, and the parish priest in *Un Baptême* (I think that is all), the most sympathetic characters in the tales. Look also at the Tellier household taken by ' Madame ' to her niece's first Communion, and the ineffable contrasts that result from it ; and Captain Sommerive's dodge to make little André disgusted with his mamma's bed, and the peculiar impression that comes from that tale (*Le Mal d'André*), of which one asks oneself whether it has a right to be comical, though it is ' terribly ' so.

There is in these stories and in some others a triumphant brutality, a determination to regard men as sad or comical animals, a large contempt for humanity, which becomes indulgent, it is true, immediately when there comes into play *divûmque hominumque voluptas, alma Venus :* all this saved in most cases by the rapidity and frankness of the narrative, by the out-and-out gaiety, by the perfect naturalness, and also (I scarcely dare say it, but it will explain itself) by the very depth of the artist's sensuality, which at least always spares us mere smuttiness.

For there is, it seems to me, a great difference between the two, and one which it is useful to point out, smuttiness being rather in the tales of former times, and sensuality in those of to-day. Smuttiness perhaps consists essentially in *playing the wit* on certain subjects ; it is the jocularity of a schoolboy or of a vicious old man ; it implies, at bottom, something forbidden and, consequently, the idea of a rule, and it is even from this that its relish comes. Sensuality ignores this rule, or forgets it ; it enjoys things frankly, and intoxicates itself with them. It is not always gay, it even readily turns into melancholy. It can be ignoble if it shuts itself up in the initial sensation, and is then the *delectatio morosa* of the theologians. But it need not be said that it never behaves thus in an artist ; on the contrary, by a natural and invincible movement it becomes poetry. It makes the whole being vibrate, stirs the imagination, and, by the feeling of what is finite and fugitive, even the understanding and the reason. Little by little the lowest sensation expands into the Pantheistic dream or refines itself into the supreme disenchantment. *Surgit amari aliquid.* Sensuality is thus something less frivolous and more æsthetic than smuttiness. Good or bad, I know not ; certainly dissolving, destructive of the will, and menacing to the moral faith.

It must be admitted that it more and more invades our own generation. The reason is, we are told, that we have more delicate nerves, more temptations in this direction, and, on the other hand, less robust beliefs, and very little power of resistance. Great minds have been attacked by this agreeable malady at the period when they are entering upon mature age, above all, those whose youth has been severe. One feels, while reading *La Femme* and *L'Amour*, that Michelet was not quite undisturbed by it. Preoccupation with women became excessive in the last writings of one of our most famous contemporaries— tell me if there is not in some passages of *La Fontaine de Jouvence* an almost avowed regret that its author had renounced his share in the banquet, a very poignant feeling of something irreparable ; on the whole, although stifled by litotes, shades of meaning, light and elusive phrases, the cry of desire and despair of old Faust recognizing that he had let slip the substance for the shadow. ' Later, I saw well the vanity of this virtue as of all others ; I recognized, in particular, that nature is not at all desirous that man should be chaste.' This declaration is of a nature to make simple persons like ourselves shudder, coming as it does from a member of the Institute. If it is true that nature ' does not desire ' what old Prospero says (and she shows it plainly enough !), I still think that society has some interest in providing that this virtue should not be too greatly dis-

credited and that it should be practised whole-
sale by individuals : perhaps it has its value,
if not in itself, at least as being ordinarily
the best and the most decisive test of the will,
for he who conquers himself in this respect
has a good deal of power over himself. But
let us not make ourselves ridiculous by moral-
izing when grandfathers are flippant. I only
beg that this is not taken for a digression ;
for in all that I have said or quoted you
can see what an advantage M. de Maupassant
can extract from it, and how innocent the
apophthegms of the sages of our time make
him out to be.

However this may be, if, when purified
and no longer more than a memory or a regret, sensualism even allies itself with the
speculations of the most delicate scepticism,
it accords still better with pessimism and
brutality in art ; for, being by nature insa-
tiable and ultimately painful and disturbing,
it does not incline to see the world in its noble
aspects, and, feeling itself fatal, it is ready to
extend to everything this fatality that is in
itself. Now, M. de Maupassant is extra-
ordinarily sensual ; he is gladly, feverishly,

and enthusiastically sensual ; he is as it were haunted by certain images, by the memory of certain sensations. It will be understood that I hesitate to bring forward here proofs of this, but read the story of Marroca, for instance, or that of the lover who kills his mistress's horse out of jealousy. You will see in glancing through these tales, that if it sometimes happens that M. de Maupassant is merely smutty or broad (and in this case he is saved by laughter), more often still he has great sensuality, that which—what shall I say ?—is not localized, but overflows everywhere and makes the physical universe its delicious prey. To the initial and crude sensations are added the impressions of surrounding objects, landscape, lines, colours, sounds, perfumes, the hour of the day or night. He enjoys odours thoroughly (see *Une Idylle, Les Sœurs Rondoli*, etc.), for in fact sensations of this sort are particularly voluptuous and enervating. But, to tell the truth, he enjoys the entire world, and in him feeling for nature and love are invoked and blended.

This manner of feeling, which is not new but is interesting in the author of so many joyous narratives, is to be found in his earliest work, in his book of verses, which is marked by so wide an inspiration and, in spite of its faults, by so ardent a poetry. Its three capital pieces are three dramas of love, in the highest degree natural, which are ended by death. What love? An irresistible force, a fatal desire which associates us with the physical universe (for desire is the soul of the world) and which leads the lovers from unsatisfied craving to sadness and from the rage for satisfaction to death (*Au Bord de l'Eau*). The author of the *Cas de Madame Luneau* began with verses that remind one of the poetry of Lucretius and the philosophy of Schopenhauer, and this is what, in fact, is at the basis of most of his tales.

Thus we see how many new elements are added to the old and eternal foundation of smuttiness—observation of reality, and more readily of dull or violent reality ; instead of the old wantonness, a profound sensuality enlarged by the feeling of nature and often blended with sadness and poetry. All these things are not encountered at the same time in all M. de Maupassant's tales. I

give the impression left by them taken as a
whole.   Amidst his robust jollities, he has
sometimes, whether natural or acquired, a
vision similar to that of Flaubert or of M.
Zola ; he also is attacked by the most recent
malady of writers, I mean pessimïsm and the
strange mania for making out the world to be
very ugly and very brutal, for showing it
governed by blind instincts, for thus almost
eliminating psychology, the good old ' study of
the human heart,' and for endeavouring at the
same time to represent in detail and with a
relief that has not yet been attained this
world which is of so little interest in itself
and only of interest as material for art ; so
that the pleasure of the writer and of those
who enjoy him and enter fully into his thought
consists only of irony, pride, and selfish
pleasure.   No concern about what used to be
be called the ideal, no preoccupation with
morality, no sympathy for men, but perhaps
a contemptuous pity for absurd and miserable
humanity ; on the other hand, a subtle skill
in enjoying the world in so far as it falls within the senses and is of a nature to gratify them ;
the interest that is refused to things themselves

fully granted to the art of reproducing them in as plastic a form as possible ; on the whole, the attitude of a misanthropical, scoffing, and lascivious god. A strange and essentially diabolical pleasure, and one in which a Port-Royalist—or perhaps, in .another department of thought, M. Barbey d'Aurevilly——would recognize an effect of original sin, a legacy from Adam's weakness and curiosity, a gift from the first rebel ! I amuse myself by speaking like a grumbling idealist, and it is probable that I stress these characteristics merely by bringing them together, but certainly this proud and voluptuous pessimism is at the foundation of a great part of the literature of to-day. Now this manner of seeing and feeling is seldom met with in the past centuries ; this neuropathic pessimism hardly exists in our classics ; why then have I said that M. Guy de Maupassant is one ?

III

He is one by his form. He joins to a vision of the world, to feelings and preferences of which the classics would not have approved, all the external qualities of classic art. Moreover, this has been also one of Flaubert's originalities ; but it seems to be more constant and less laborious in M. de Maupassant.

' Classical qualities, classical form,' are easy words to say. What exactly do they mean ? They imply an idea of excellence ; they imply also clearness, sobriety, the art of composition ; they mean, finally, that reason, rather than imagination and sensibility, presides over the execution of the work, and that the writer dominates his material.

M. de Maupassant dominates his material marvellously, and it is through this that he is a master. From the first he has conquered us by qualities which we enjoyed all the more as they are regarded as characteristics of our natural genius, as we found them where we had not dreamed of expecting them, and as, besides, they gave us a rest from the tiring affectations of other writers. In three or four years he became famous, and it is a long time since a literary reputation has been established so suddenly. His verses date from 1880. It was at once felt that there was more in *Venus Rustique* than the evidence of a very warm temperament. Then came *Boule-de-Suif*, that wonder. At the same time M. Zola informed us in an article that the author was as vigorous as his style, and this pleased us. Since then M. de Maupassant has not ceased to write with facile pen his compact little masterpieces.

His prose is excellent, so clear, so direct, so unstudied! He has, like everybody to-day, skilful conjunctions of words, lucky hits in expression, but they are always so natural with him, so pat to the subject, and so spontaneous that one only notices this too late. Notice also the fullness, the good disposition of his phrasing, when it happens to stretch out a little, and how it falls back ' squarely ' on its feet. His verses, although their poetry was vigorous and abundant, were rather the verses of a writer of prose (a little like those of Alfred de Musset). This was recognizable by various signs, for instance, by the slight attention which he gives to the rhyme, the scant care he takes to improve it, and also by this, that the phrase moves and develops independently of the system of rhymes or of the strophe, and con-

tinually overflows it. Here are the first
verses in the volume :

' Les fenêtres étaient ouvertes. Le salon
  Illuminé jetait des lueurs d'incendies,
  Et de grandes clartés couraient sur le gazon.
  Le parc là-bas semblait répondre aux mélodies
  De l'orchestre, et faisait une rumeur au loin.' [1]

The first four lines form, by the arrangement of the rhymes, a quatrain which the
end of the phrase passes over, bringing in a
fresh rhyme ; there is thus a sort of overflow
from one strophe to the next. All through
the collection something difficult to specify
betrays in the poet the vocation of a writer
of prose.

Classic by the naturalness of his prose, by
the good standard of his vocabulary, and by
the simplicity of the rhythm of his phrases,
M. de Maupassant is classical also by the
quality of his comedy. I am afraid I have
strangely blackened him a moment ago.
Let us only say that his gaiety is not light ;
that as things often have two sides (without

[1] ' The windows were open. The illuminated drawing-
room threw forth a blaze of lights, and great beams ran
over the turf. The park beneath seemed to answer the
melodies of the orchestra, and uttered a distant murmur.'

counting the others), those with which he is
accustomed to make us laugh are hardly less
lamentable than ridiculous, and, in a word,
that what is or appears to be comic is almost
always, in the final analysis, some deformity
or some moral or physical suffering. But
this species of cruelty in laughter would be
found in the greatest and most admired of
laughers. And then there are also many of
his tales which are purely droll and leave no
after-taste. In brief, if M. de Maupassant
is more than moderately brutal, he is also
more than moderately gay. And his comedy
comes from the things themselves and from the
situations ; it does not reside in the narrator's
style nor in his wit. M. de Maupassant has
never been witty, and perhaps never will be,
in the sense in which the world is understood
by men about town. But he has the gift by
plainly telling stories, without hits, without
witticisms, without efforts, without contor-
tions, of exciting unmeasured gaieties and
bursts of inextinguishable laughter. Read
again only *Boule-de-Suif*, *La Maison Tellier*,
La Rouille, *Le Remplacant*, *Décoré*, *La Pa-
tronne*, the end of *Les Sœurs Rondoli*, or the

episode of Lesable and the handsome Maze in *L'Héritage.* Now, there you have great art employed on little subjects, and, as nothing is more classical than to obtain powerful effects by very simple means, you will find that the epithet of classic is not out of place.

M. de Maupassant displays extreme clearness in his narratives and in the drawing of his characters. He distinguishes and brings into relief, with a great power of simplification and singular sureness of touch, the essential features in the physiognomy of his characters. Some obstinate psychologist may say : 'That is not surprising, for there is nothing complex about them. And he only paints them from without, by their behaviour and their acts ! ' Well, what would you have ? The soul of Madame Luneau or that of Gaffer Omont is, in truth, very simple, and fine shades and conflicts and delicate confusions of ideas and feelings are seldom encountered in the regions that please M. de Maupassant. But what of this ? The world is thus constructed, and we cannot all be like Obermann, Horace, or Madame de Mortsauf. And I would say here, if this were the place to say it, that psychological analysis is not perhaps so great a mystery as is thought. ' But Miss Harriet, sir ? How comes she to love that young painter ? What a blend that love must make with this young lady's other feelings ! Her past history, her sufferings, her internal struggles—these are what would be interesting.' I think, alas ! that they would be very commonplace, and that Miss Harriet amuses us and remains in our memory precisely because she is only an odd, ridiculous, and touching silhouette. There is in all these tales just as much ' psychology ' as they need. There is some in *La Ficelle* ; there is some of another sort in *Le Réveil*, and, if you require a singular combination of feelings mingled with rare sensations (something like Pierre Loti, but with a few more verbs and less adjectives), you will find a specimen of it in that pretty fantasy, *Châli*.

M. de Maupassant has yet another merit, which, without being confined to the classics, is more frequently found in them and is becoming rather rare with us. He has in the highest degree the art of composition, the art of subordinating all else to something that is essential, to an idea, to a situation, so that in the first place everything prepares for it, and that afterwards everything contributes to render it more striking and to draw out all its effects. Hence none of those digressions which abound in so many other ' sensitive ' writers who do not control themselves, and who like to slip through any opening they find. Just as much description or landscape as is needed ' to give the setting ' as the phrase runs; and descriptions themselves very well composed, not made up of details of equal value interminably heaped up together, but brief and taking from things only those features that stand out and give an epitome of the whole. This very frank art can be studied in fairly long narratives like *Boule-de-Suif*, *En Famille*, *Un Héritage*. But look how in *Ce Cochon de Morin* the first page prepares for, explains, and justifies the poor man's folly; then look how everything contributes to give humour to the exclamation which is regularly repeated, ' that pig, Morin '; how all the details of Henrietta's seduction by Labarbe make the repetition more unexpected, more delicious, invest it, so to speak, with more and more force and irony, and how deep and irresistible its humour appears, at the very end, in the mouth of Henrietta's husband. Clear, simple, connected, and vigorous, succulent in their deep-seated drollery, such are almost all these little tales ; and how rapid is their action !

It is rather curious that, of all the story-tellers and novelists who have a vogue to-day, it should be perhaps the most daring and the most indecent who approaches closest to the sober perfection of the venerable classics ; that one is able to observe in *Boule-de-Suif* the application of the excellent rules inscribed in books of rhetoric, and that *L'Histoire d'une Fille de Ferme*, though it may alarm their modesty, is of a sort to satisfy those humanists who are best furnished with precepts and doctrines. And yet this is the case. One can doubtless show M. de Maupassant's relation to some of his contemporaries. Manifestly he proceeds from Flaubert : he has often, with more gaiety, the style of irony of that old pessimist, and, with more ease, his fixed and precise form. From M. Zola, with less sombre morosity and a less epic gait, he has a fond-

ness for certain brutalities. And lastly, there
is something in him which makes one think
at times of a Paul de Kock who could write.
A professor of my acquaintance (who defined Plutarch as ' the La Bruyère apostle of a
Pagan confessional ') would not hesitate to call
M. de Maupassant a sober and light-hearted
Zola, an easy and relaxed Flaubert, an artistic and misanthropical Paul de Kock. But
what does this mean except that he is himself, with a fund of feelings and ideas by
which he is of his own time, and with qualities
of form by which he makes us think of the
old masters, and avoids the fashionable affectations, preciosity, jargon, obscurity, ver-
bosity, and contempt for composition ?

Need I now say that, although a faultless
sonnet is as good as a long poem, a short
story is doubtless a cheaper masterpiece than
a novel ; that, moreover, in M. de Maupassant's tales one would find, by making a
careful search, some faults, especially forced
effects, and here and there excesses of style
(as when, in order to obtain a stronger effect,
he shows us in *La Maison Tellier* children who
are making their first Communion ' thrown

on the flagstones by a burning devotion ' and
' shivering with a divine fever '—this in the
country ! in a Norman village ! little Nor-
mans !) ? Need I add that one cannot have
everything, and that I cannot at all imagine
him writing *La Princesse de Clèves* or even
Adolphe ? Assuredly also there are things
which one is allowed to love as much as the
Contes de la Bécasse. One may even prefer
to the author of *Marroca* some artist at once
less classic and less brutal, and love him, I
suppose, for the very refinement and distinction of his faults. But M. de Maupassant
remains a writer almost irreproachable in a
literary form that is not irreproachable, so
well is he able to disarm the austere and
doubly to please those who are not austere.

PIERRE LOTI

I HAVE just read over again, almost without pause, in the country, huddled close to mother earth, beneath an enervating thunder-laden sky, Pierre Loti's six volumes. Now, as I turn over the last page, I feel a sense of complete intoxication. I am full of the sad and delicious memory of a prodigious quantity of most profound sensations, and my heart is filled with a vague and universal tenderness. To speak, if I can, with more precision, those two thousand pages have suggested to me, have made me imagine too great a number of unexpected perceptions, and those perceptions were accompanied by too much pleasure and, at the same time, by too much pain, too much pity, too many indefinite and unrealizable desires. My soul is like an instrument that has vibrated overmuch, and to which the mute prolongation of past vibrations is painful. I would like to enjoy and suffer the entire earth, the totality of life, and, like St. Anthony at the end of his temptation, to embrace the world.

You can, if you like, regard this impression which those novels leave upon me as excessive. I myself confess that my critical conscience is perturbed. The greatest masterpieces of literature have never troubled me thus. What is there then in those stories of Loti? For they are composed with extreme negligence, written in a restricted vocabulary, in little, closely-constructed phrases. You will find in them neither extraordinary or powerful dramas, nor subtle analyses of character, for everything is reduced to love affairs followed by separations, the characters in which have very simple souls. Many books, both old and recent, presuppose a far higher effort of thought, invention, and execution. But, in spite of this, Loti's novels take possession of me and oppress me more than a drama of Shakspere, a tragedy of Racine, or a novel of Balzac. And it is for this reason that I am perturbed. Have they some witchcraft in them, some sorcery, some charm which is inexplicable or only explicable by something other than their literary merits ?

For these novels move the soul at once in all in it that is most refined and in all in it that is most elementary. They strike, if I may use the phrase, both extremes of the key-board of sentiment. For, on the one hand, you have under your eyes the most singular objects, you receive from them the newest, the rarest, and the sharpest impressions ; and, on the other hand, you have experienced the most natural feelings, those most completely human, those accessible to all. You, with your eyes of a Western dilettante in love with the picturesque, have seen the *upa-upa* danced in Tahiti ; you have seen Burmese dancers who look like bats . . . ; and you have wept for old women, dying children, or parting lovers with the best part of your soul, the part of you that is simplest and healthiest, with the same heart as that with which you love your mother or your country. You have known the agitations of the most inquisitive and most experienced sensuality—and the emotions of the purest sympathy and the chastest pity.

Thus you enjoy in those books the limpid charm of ingenuous poems and the perverse charm of the last investigations of contemporary æstheticism—that which is at the beginning of literatures and that which is at their end. A page communicates to you two distinct impressions between which there are thousands of years—and between which there is sometimes also ‘ the frightful thickness of the world.’ And little by little the poet insinuates within you his own soul, a soul that seems contemporary with humanity at its birth and in its old age, that seems to have traversed the entire surface of the terrestrial globe ; a soul amorous and sad, always restless and always quivering. And it is this soul that gives Loti’s little phrases their immense power to make you tremble.

One can see from Loti’s example how it is, and by what path, old literatures sometimes return to absolute simplicity. An extreme artistic sensibility employed upon the most extraordinary objects and finally resting in the translation of the simplest feelings ; what is called ‘ impressionism ’ resulting in a purely natural poetry—such is almost the case of the

author of *Aziyadé* and *Pêcheur d'Islande*.
Now, on looking a little more closely, we
think we see that it is the ' exoticism' of the
objects which first occupied it that has
sharpened his sensibility to this point, and
that it is certain feelings engendered by this
exoticism which have led it back to the fine
simplicity of the idylls or the familiar tragedies.
Let us see how this singular evolution has
been accomplished.

I

Unique circumstances have contributed to
form Pierre Loti's talent. After a dreamy
and tender childhood, he became a pupil of
the Naval School, and then wandered over
the world. Think what an effect this sailor's
life, so different from ours, can have upon the
soul. During long voyages, in the infinite
solitude of the sea, the persistent idea and
feeling of the immensity of the universe and
the fatality of natural forces must slowly fill
you with an indefinable sadness. And, if this
feeling can in some people turn into a grave
piety, it can just as easily resolve itself into
a resigned fatalism. Then the profound

diversity of human beings on the different points of the globe, the multiplicity of religions, moralities, and customs, is certainly not an encouragement to belief. Finally, the long isolations and abstinences of the seaman are interspersed by hours of folly and retaliation, when his starved senses rush to their satisfaction. All those journeys through the world, interminable reveries, and violent orgies are equally calculated to exasperate the sensibility and to empty the soul of any positive faith. At the age of twenty-seven, Pierre Loti, who had dreamed on all oceans and visited all the places of pleasure in the universe, writes quietly, among other pretty things, to his friend, William Brown :

> ' Believe me, my poor friend, time and debauchery are two great remedies. . . . There is no God ; there is no morality ; nothing exists of all that we have been taught to respect ; there is a passing life from which it is logical to ask for the greatest possible amount of enjoyment while we await the final terror which is death. . . . I am going to open my heart to you, to make to you my pro-

fession of faith. My rule of conduct is always to do what I like in spite of all morality and all social conventions. I believe in nothing and in nobody; I do not love anybody or anything; I have neither faith nor hope.'

You will say : ' Those remarks are a little lacking in novelty; all this is the most venerable romanticism; Loti speaks here like Lara, Manfred, and the Corsair, a bit more brutally, and that is all.' Yes, but Pierre Loti, fortunately brought up outside of literature, is here Byronian without knowing it and with entire sincerity. He begins over again, on his own account, the moral evolution of his century. And Pierre Loti has gone the right way to work by passing through absolute despair and negation ; for, from that moment onwards, he goes through the world with no other care than that of collecting the strongest and most delicate sensations. He no longer regards the visible universe as anything except a prey offered to his imagination and his senses. And this great writer-to-be assigns to himself a life more and more different from that of the professional writer

and man of letters. How puny and wretched
a life, in truth, is that of the scribe engaged
in his corner in polishing his phrases and
noting down his little observations about a
tiny human group, when the world is so vast
and humanity so varied ! Loti hardens his
muscles, makes his body agile, supple, and
robust, the body of a gymnast or a clown.
He adorns that body richly, and disguises it
in a hundred ways. He finds in this the
pleasure of a child or of a savage. He forms
close friendships with handsome and primitive
beings, Samuel, Achmet, Ives, creatures more
noble and elegant than common-place civilized
persons, beings with whom his mind has not
to force or restrain itself, and with whom it
also enjoys the pleasure of absolute domina-
tion. He enjoys the inexhaustible variety of
the aspects of the earth, and, perhaps still
more, all that is unexpected in the human
animal. He enjoys feeling that between
certain races there are differences so great
that they will never understand one another,
feeling that men are impenetrable and unintelligible to one another just as the universe
is unintelligible to them all. He loves women

of all types and of all forms of beauty in all
the countries in the world—Aziyadé, Rarahu,
Pasquala, Fatougaye—and on each occasion
he knows the pride and delight of being
absolutely loved, even to the death. In this
way he accomplishes his dream—to enjoy
with his whole body and to enjoy throughout
the whole extent of the planet on which that
body has been thrown. For is it not a pity
that, being able to know the entire earth and
in this way to multiply our life and our being,
we should remain shut up in our own little
rabbit-hutch? Very really we can say that
Loti's dream of life is very superior to ours,
and that the world is a very different place
to him and to us who remain motionless. He
is one of those rare men who have lived in a
whole planet ; I shall die having only lived
in a town, or at the most, in a province.
Pierre Loti's life seems to me so fine that, in
order to prevent myself from thinking of it
with bitterness and envy, I need to recall
these words in the *Imitation of Jesus Christ:*
' What canst thou see elsewhere, which thou
seest not where thou art ? Behold the
heavens and the earth and all the elements ;

for of these are all things' made. . . . If
thou couldst see all things at once before thee,
what would it be but an empty show ? '
(Book I. Chap. XX.) But even this does
not suffice to console me .

II

Now, one day, whilst he was leading this
extraordinary life, Pierre Loti took it into
his head to note down his impressions for his
own pleasure. And this naval officer, who,
if one is to believe the story, was almost
ignorant of contemporary literature, who had
not read a page of Flaubert, or of the Goncourts, or of Daudet, forthwith revealed himself as one of the foremost of our writers and
one of the most surprising painters of exotic
subjects that we have ever seen.

It is true, indeed, that everything seemed
to conspire to make Pierre Loti's exoticism
something very penetrating and very powerful.

I do not believe that it is much more than
a hundred years since exoticism made its
entrance into our literature. It presupposes
a gift which is not entirely developed until
very late in blind and routine-ridden humanity

—the gift of *seeing* and loving the physical universe in all its details. This gift is very slight in men of primitive times and of the middle ages of civilizations. They see things exactly, but they see them summarily. The men of the Middle Ages discovered the East, that is to say a nature, a humanity, and an art, very different from their own, though they hardly seem to have suspected it; almost nothing of this strangeness and picturesqueness has passed into the *chansons de geste* that followed the Crusades nor into the *fabliaux*. It is not a paradox, I assure you, to say that it is only in our own days that man has had eyes, has been able to see the external world in its entirety. If some poets had not come who were endowed with singular faculties, humanity would have been for ever ignorant of the appearance of its own planet. It was, I think, Bernardin de Saint-Pierre, that great vagabond, that bold and tender genius, who began to see. He was the first whose perception was moved by the flora of the tropics. And it was the novelty of a foreign region which unsealed his eyes and allowed him to open them afterwards upon nature as she is among ourselves ; and thus it was exoticism which definitely introduced the picturesque into our literature. Then Chateaubriand described America, its virgin forests, its pampas, and its great rivers. And then appeared romanticism, whose principal function it is to describe what we are not accustomed to see—Spain, Italy, the East, and the Middle Ages, for distance in time is equivalent to distance in space. Doubtless romanticism is often lacking in sincerity ; it descends to conventionalities, to gewgaws, and trinkets. There is much to criticize in the East of the *Orientales* and in the Middle Ages of *Notre-Dame de Paris*. No matter ; the faculty of seeing and profoundly enjoying forms and aspects of things has been awakened and will never sleep again. And on the day that this faculty applies itself no longer to foreign objects, but to what is under our eyes every day, a new literature is born ; romanticism engenders naturalism. But, however interesting descriptions of reality close to us may be, exoticism, when it is sincere, preserves a special charm, at once penetrating and saddening. For proof I only require some pages of *Salammbô*, Fromentin's two volumes *Sahel* and *Sahara*, and the novels of Pierre Loti, that king of exoticism.

Everything, as I have said, seems to have conspired to secure this sovereignty to the author of *Aziyadé*. At least three conditions were necessary. It was a good thing, in the first place, that the writer should see the entire world, not only the Pacific but the Polar Seas, not only America but China, not only Tahiti but Senegal. For if he had only known one or two regions, he would run the risk of confining himself to describing only them, and of repeating continually with artifice what he would have done at first with sincerity. His sensibility should, moreover, in order to become more sharpened and rejuvenated, employ itself upon objects as diverse as possible. Now the complete inspection of this immense universe was hardly permissible and easy except to a man of the end of this century. Pierre Loti has had the good sense to be born in it—and to be a naval officer, that is to say, condemned by his profession to endless wanderings. It was necessary, in the second place, that the writer should know how to see. That is not so common, at least in the degree in which this gift was needed in the case we are discussing. I have said that it is only a century since the superior section of humanity began properly to grasp the marvellous diversity of its habitation. Even to-day simple people and three-quarters of cultivated men do not see. I have often questioned peasants who had been soldiers in the marine infantry, who had lived in China, in Tonkin, in the Antilles, in Senegal ; I assure you they saw nothing. And the good missionaries, preoccupied with a single idea, haunted by their dream of evangelization, saw 'foreign lands' scarcely better. Besides, if they had seen them properly, they would no longer have courage for action, for then they would understand the abyss that separates races, and they would abandon their sublime and impossible task. Now, Pierre Loti has in an eminent degree the gift of seeing and feeling. He accounts for it in *Aziyadé* with a little effort and some pedantry ; but this very effort of expression is an assurance that he knows the inestimable rarity of the gift that is in him :

' You are impressed by a succession of sounds ; you hear a melodic phrase that pleases you. Why does it please you ? Because the musical intervals of which the succession is composed, in other words the relations between the numbers of the vibrations of the sonorous bodies, are expressed by certain figures rather than by others. Change those figures and your sympathy is no longer excited ; you say that it is no longer musical, that it is a succession of incoherent sounds. Several simultaneous sounds are heard ; you receive an impression which will be pleasant or painful— a matter of the relations of figures, which are the sympathetic relations between an external phenomenon and yourself, a sensitive being.

' There are real affinities between you and certain successions of sounds, between you and certain bright colours, between you and certain luminous reflections, between you and certain lines, certain forms. Although the relations of harmony between all those different things and yourself are too complicated to be expressed as in the case of music, yet you feel that they exist. . . .

'All this being granted, let us pass to the definition of you, Loti. There is an affinity between all orders of things and you. You are of a nature very eager for artistic and intellectual enjoyments, and you can only be happy in the midst of all that is able to satisfy your sympathetic needs, which are immense.'

Lastly, it is necessary that the writer should be able to express what he has seen and felt. How many men have had rare impressions and original visions, of whom we shall never know anything because they were powerless to translate them into words ! Pierre Loti has found himself in possession of this supreme gift of expression. And, as he has grown freely, outside of all literary schools, it has been given him to have at once the sharpness of perception of the subtlest of his contemporaries and something of the simplicity of form of the primitive writers. This case is perhaps unique. What would you say of a Homer who had the feelings of Edmond de Goncourt ?

III

Here my embarrassment redoubles. How am I to get close enough to this wizard, Pierre Loti, and define him with any precision ? He is first of all in the very things that the writer places under our eyes. We very easily allow ourselves to be captured by exoticism. It was by exoticism that *Paul et Virginie* a century ago, and *Atala* since then, seized so powerfully upon the public imagination. Men of the people and simple-minded folk adore romances that speak to them of things they have not seen, of lagoons and gondolas, or that present them with vignettes of the East, with caravans, minarets, and yataghans. For us there is a less vulgar charm, but one of the same species, in Pierre Loti's descriptions. In the first place, they flatter the desire for novelty that we have within us. And these evocations of objects to which our senses are not accustomed move us all the more keenly. Then, those unknown things, those combinations hitherto unexperienced of

lines, colours, sounds, and perfumes, give us
the impression of something distant and
fugitive, remind us that the world is large,
and that we never grasp more than tiny portions of it at the same time. And, finally,
while we imagine new aspects of the universe,
it happens that as soon as we have well
entered into these visions, we find ourselves
ill at ease and vaguely anxious among them,
we feel a homesick regret for known and
familiar visions whose familiarity has rendered
them reassuring to us.

Thus there is something delicious and
melancholy in exoticism. It enchants us like
a Paradise and depresses us like exile. But
this melancholy and this délight are of a
peculiar intensity in Pierre Loti. Why?
Quite simply (it is always necessary to return
to this point), because he feels more profoundly than we do, and because he represents
his sensations with more sincerity or more
directly, or arranges them less. He fears
neither disorder nor repetitions ; there are
only primitive methods and no ' manner ' in
his style. Continually, when he despairs of
being able to render an impression in its

entirety, he ingeniously employs the words
' strange,' ' inexpressible,' ' indefinable.' But
these words with him are never empty of
meaning ; his pictures are so precise that these
vague words, so far from weakening them,
finish them, and carry them on in a dreamy
prolongation. And I need not say that his
descriptions are never purely external, that
he habitually notes down at the same time
the sensation and the feeling which it excites
in him, and that this feeling is always very
strong and very sad. But what is peculiar
to him is that sensations and feelings usually
resolve themselves into a sort of languor of
voluptuousness and desire, as if the trouble
that the face of the Earth awakens within
him were similar to another trouble, to that
which comes from woman, and fills the whole
soul and body.

All this is very difficult to say clearly.
What is certain is that a mortal languor
exhales from every page of the *Mariage de
Loti*. Tahiti, so far away, has the sorrowful
attraction of a sensual, inaccessible Paradise
to which we shall never go. A land of Eden
whose fauna and flora are all friendly, where

there are neither poisons nor serpents, where
men neither labour nor toil, where laughing
little girls spend their lives crowning themselves with flowers and sporting naked in
clear pools into which lemons and oranges
fall. Humanity there is eternally childlike.
The very notion of sin is absent. Theft,
cupidity, ambition, and all the vices that
spring from it are unknown there, for the
earth nurtures men without toil, and the
struggle for life is not even imagined. The
stain of the flesh is unknown there, and also,
as a consequence, modesty, which Milton
calls immodest. There the influence of the
earth, the sweetness of things, perfumes, the
beauty of nature and the beauty of the body,
the cooling breezes of evening, call so clearly
and invincibly to love that in doing so they
give absolution for it, and no one thinks of
attaching to it any idea of defilement. This
world is the world before the Law, for the
Law has made sin, as St. Paul says. All
duties there are but natural charity, kindness,
and pity. One is enervated there by the
blessedness of being alive, and the abundance
and continuity of agreeable sensations lull

you to sleep in an endless dream. But at the same time the old world makes strange and sudden appearances in this childlike isle at which its ships stop in passing. And the old world is doubtless sin, but it is also effort ; it is moral pain, but it is dignity ; it is labour, but it is intelligence. And then the delights of the Paradisaical isle assume for the man of the old world the savour of forbidden fruit. He has a vague fear of this garden of the Pacific where man does not suffer. And the question stirs obscurely within him : Which is the better, this delicious, innocent, insignificant, and puerile life, or the other life, the life of the West, that which has vice and evil, effort and virtue ? He is disconcerted by this sudden disappearance of pain in a lost island, nine thousand miles from Paris and London. Has he reached another planet ? And what also increases his trouble is the mystery of that Maori race which comes one knows not whence, which passes its life in dreaming and making love, which has for its whole religion only a vague belief in the spirits of the dead ; of that voluptuous and dreamy race which lives in natural surroundings so beautiful but mute, where there are no birds, where one only hears the noise of the waves and of the wind ; of that race with no history which continues to diminish and die out year by year, and which will die of having been too happy. . . . And yet Queen Pomaré gives a ball in her drawing-room to the naval officers. One of them sits at the piano and plays Chopin. The queen is wearing a red velvet dress. European things and Polynesian things are in a wild contrast. And outside, in the gardens, young girls clothed in muslin are singlng choruses, just as in Utopia or Atlantis ; then the dances begin, lascivious and furious, which, as the dawn comes, end with a universal festival of the flesh. . . . Put all those impressions together, and other indefinable ones also, which I forget, and you will understand that there is nothing more sensual, more languishing, more melancholy than the *Mariage de Loti*.

Aziyadé troubles you in another way. In the first place by the impression of strange voluptuousness that proceeds from it, profound and absorbed voluptuousness, without thought or speech. That bed of love, at night, on a boat, in the Gulf of Salonica ; then that life of silence and solitude, for a year, in an old house in the oldest quarter of Constantinople—I know no sweeter or more enervating dream, nor one in which the conscience and the will are more lulled to sleep. And this is not all. Pierre Loti has been able to rejuvenate what is familiar and hackneyed in Turkish life. How ? By becoming a Turk, by assuming for a year the soul of an effendi. I do not think there has ever been seen in an artist a finer effort of the sympathetic imagination, such a fixed determination to allow his soul to be moulded by external influences as if it were infinitely impressionable and malleable material, and, with that end, to limit his life to sensations ; nor, on the other hand, so marvellous an aptitude for tasting them all. That is extraordinary and a little disconcerting. We are in the presence of a soul that has so thoroughly delivered itself as a prey to the external world that it is capable of living all lives and that it lends itself to all sorts of incarnations. In truth, has Pierre Loti a soul of his own ? Perhaps he has several, perhaps what is most

intimate and deepest in him really changes as
he changes his place of abode. He makes us
feel our profound dependence on the visible
world ; he would make us doubt our own
personality and talk the most far-fetched
nonsense about the enigma of the ' ego.'

In the *Roman d'un Spahi* the general
impression is cruel. Pierre Loti shows us
this time the unfriendly aspects of the earth.
The landscape in that book is, of all landscapes, the most sterile, the most hostile to
man, the most desolate, beneath its blinding
sun the most lugubrious. There are tawny,
boundless sands, stained with frightful negro
villages like leprous sores, or marshes full of
poisons which ooze horribly at sunset. And
humanity is at its most wretched, most
brutal, closest to the beasts. And there are
also black loves, and, on certain days, howling
dances of ebony bodies let loose by an animal
Venus. There is the grimacing visage of
Fatou-gaye who looks both like a monkey and
like a little girl. . . . There are, in turn,
depressing boredom and furious pleasure
beneath the weight of the blazing sky. And
you recollect the abominable culmination—

the battle between the Spahis and the negroes, the death of Jean, of Fatou-gaye, and of their child, that hideous splash of blood in the dim light of the tangle of giant vegetation which in itself has also a venomous and ferocious air.

IV

From this voluptuous and sad exoticism there issue certain very great, very simple, and eternal feelings which prolong and deepen the sensations noted down. There is, in the first place, the ever-present feeling of the immensity of the world. One can say that the total image of the earth is obscurely evoked by each of Loti's landscapes ; for each landscape holds us only because it is new to us, and because we feel that it is separated from us by unmeasured spaces. Now this feeling brings with it a certain melancholy : through it we clearly know our own littleness, and that we shall never be able to enjoy all the universe at once. And this idea of the size of the earth is still more increased by that of its duration. Into Pierre Loti's descriptions there often slip geological visions, recollections of the history of the globe. A night of calm on the equatorial sea gives him the impression that in the first ages ' before light was separated from darkness, things must have had this tranquil attitude of expectation ; the repose between the creations must have had those periods of inexpressible immobility.' The Icelandic sea has for him ' aspects of non-life, of a finite or as yet uncreated world.' The landscapes of Brittany give him the effect of primitive landscapes, such as they were three thousand years ago. But immediately, while he thinks of the earth's overwhelming vastness and duration, he feels that it is small and ephemeral, for what is it all since it is not infinite and eternal ? The incurable feeling of the vanity of things insinuates itself into his most vivid pictures. Each moment the idea of death clouds them over. It arises naturally, spontaneous and naked, and its effect is always very powerful, for, try as we may, nothing is sadder, or more alarming, or more incomprehensible than death. Lastly, this familiarity with the vast spectacles of nature and of the melancholy into which they plunge us, brings forcibly with it a certain contempt for all that attracts and engages sedentary writers, for the narrow civilizations and the depressing and artificial life of European cities. The minute study of the vices of some city-dweller has little attraction when one has the earth for one's own. Subjects with which Balzac was deeply enamoured seem paltry and without interest to the man who has traversed five continents and the entire surface of the planet.

But, moreover, it is the very exoticism of his romances that guided Pierre Loti to simple subjects and elementary dramas, and imposed them upon him. The subjects could hardly be other than stories of love with the women of the different countries which the poet has traversed—a sensual and dreamy love, an absolute love in the woman ; a curious, proud, and sometimes cruel love in the man. The drama is the simplest and most painful of all —the unique, eternal drama of the separation of beings who love one another. Thus exoticism explains, in Pierre Loti's novels, alike the novelty and intensity of the sensations, and the universal and largely human character of the feelings.

And this is why, when the seeker for

exoticism and rare impressions stops in the land of France, he can only relate to us idylls, more poignant, doubtless, but as little complicated as *Paul et Virginie*, *Graziella*, or even the episode of Nausicaa in the exquisite *Odyssey*. For not only has his wandering life made him especially acquainted with the common people and sailors, but also the satiety of personal impressions, the misanthropy that is born from excess of experience, and the very clear feeling, in the case of a man who has lived apart from cities, of what is artificial, wretched, and useless in our civilizations, make him love and embrace with ardent sympathy simple beings, more primitive and finer than we are, closer to that earth over which he has travelled and which he adores. Certainly, I love Pierre Loti's novels for many other reasons ; but I love them also for this idea with which they are deeply impregnated, that a fisherman's or a Breton peasant's soul has a thousand chances of being more interesting, more worthy of close examination, than that of a general officer, a merchant, or a politician. If I cannot be one of those privileged beings who are called artists,

who reflect within themselves and describe
what moves on the surface of the earth, I
prefer to be one of those who live close to it
and who have hardly left it.

Pêcheur d'Islande is also, like *Loti*, like the
Spahi, like *Aziyadé*, the story of a love and a
separation ; the story of the fisherman Yann
and of the good and serious Gaud who love
one another and marry, of Yann who goes
away and does not return, and of an old
woman whose grandson is going to die away
' on the other side of the earth.' *Mon Frère
Yves* is the story of a sailor who gets drunk
whenever he goes on land, who marries and
becomes a father, and who will reform perhaps ; and it is the story of the strange and
touching friendship between this sailor and
Pierre Loti. And I have nothing to say of
these two narratives except that they are
marvellously picturesque, that their emotion
is penetrating, and their simplicity absolute.
In *Pêcheur d'Islande* there are fishing and the
Polar seas ; in *Mon Frère Yves*, life on ship-
board, the seas of the East and of the tropics,
and ' the great monotony ' of the Ocean ; in
both books Brittany, its countenance and its

soul. It is also an effect of exoticism that, after having visited the world, you see again your own country and familiar objects with new and virgin eyes, with the same freshness of impression, the same astonishment, as you have seen the Congo or Tahiti. But *Mon Frère Yves* and *Pêcheur d'Islande* are two novels whose simplicity would require too difficult an effort to analyse and define, and I have only desired to show how Loti's first three novels, those rare works, were preparing for these two masterpieces.

V

I am still troubled. I am afraid that I have not been able to convey the impression that these books make upon me, and I am also afraid that I may be blamed for having tried to convey that impression. I shall be told : ' All these novels of Loti's are very negligently composed.' Is it my fault if that does not affect me ? Or : ' Do you not find too many curios and trinkets in this exoticism, too much day-dreaming, too much about coral necklaces, mangroves, cholas, and diguhelas ? We cannot verify the accu-

racy of these paintings; this abundance of
details is comparable with nothing that we
know.' Shall I say that I am childish enough
to find a charm in mysterious words ? Moreover there are not so very many of them.
Or : ' Does not nature rather overwhelm man
in those novels ? That would have been M.
Saint-Marc Girardin's opinion. Would you
not like there to be a little more psychology ? '
Why ? I find in them quite as much as I
need, and I find it of the sort that it ought to
be. ' But why do you not say, for instance,
that Pierre Loti proceeds from Musset and
from Flaubert ? And why do you not attempt
to assign him his rank in contemporary literature ? ' Alas ! I am so little of a critic that
when a writer takes hold of me I am entirely
his ; and as another will perhaps take quite
as great a hold of me, even to the extent of
almost effacing my former impressions, and
as those various impressions are never of the
same sort, I can neither compare them nor
state that the latter writer is superior to the
former. ' But we do not want to know the
emotions that books give you ; it is upon their
value that we desire to be instructed.' I am

here all the more incapable of rising above feeling, as Pierre Loti is, I think, the most delicate machine for giving sensations that I have ever met. He gives me too much pleasure and too acute a pleasure, and one which is too deeply sunken in my flesh for me to be in a condition to judge him. I am scarcely able to say that I love him.

HIPPOLYTE TAINE

HE is very great. His is perhaps the brain of this century which has stored away most facts and arranged them with most vigour. Each of his ' histories,' each of his ' descriptions '—description of a man, of a literature, of an art, of a society, of an epoch, of a country—resemble massive and serried constructions. Beneath the propositions that are linked together, the series of facts control one another—like the successive layers of a monument. Taine is a prodigious builder of pyramids.

No one has more sternly applied, nor to more varied objects, more narrowly determinist theories. But the experience of the most scholarly man being always very restricted, every explanation of any rather considerable mass of phenomena, inevitably becomes creation. The mind begins by accommodating itself to the portions of reality on which it has been able to seize, but as soon as a more extended reality or all reality is in question, it is this which we accommodate to our mind ; it is our mind which completes the facts, and which moulds them, and which supposes relations to exist between them in order to justify certain laws. All philosophy is poetry.

And this is why no one, more often than Taine, has done something different from what he believed he was doing ; no one has more felt and imagined, when he believed he was merely perceiving, observing, and classifying.

The theory which is reputed to be the buttress of *L'Histoire de la Littérature Anglaise* only accounts for the mediocre individuals; consequently it only throws light upon what interests us least. It hardly explains the great writers. Whilst Taine labours to see in them the products of the race, the environment, and the moment, he shows them to us, above all, as the producers of a certain sort of beauty to which we shall never know how much is contributed by the race, the environment, and the moment. *L'Histoire de la Littérature Anglaise* is a splendid book ; but the best part of it would remain if the theory were taken away or reduced to some rather modest truisms.

Similarly, ' the mistress faculty ' explains everything in an artist's work, except beauty. 'The mistress faculty' can, in fact, be met with as well in a ' glutton ' as in a man of genius.

In history also, Taine is often a dupe. His determinist conception inevitably leads to gloomy results, whatever be the country or time that he studies. For he always goes back in his analysis to causes that are confused with animal instinct. This is why he has seen both the old system and the Revolution to be equally sad and hateful. Decomposed in the same manner, the Middle Ages and antiquity would none the less surely have appeared hideous to him. Even the beauty of the age of Pericles, if Taine had been able to rummage among the Athenian archives, would not have been able to withstand that operation. The whole destiny of humanity is summed up for him in the sombre picture which Thomas Graindorge paints for his nephew's instructions. (Little rabbits, big elephants—do you remember it ?)

He deforms facts by this alone that he co-ordinates them without knowing them all. He is very little of an evolutionist, for his mechanical system claims to exclude mystery, and there is mystery in ' evolution.' He forgets the fluctuation, the vagueness, the want of precision, the flight and transformation of things. He immobilizes the real in order to observe it, so that what he observes is no longer the real. Assuredly Jacobin and Napoleonic institutions are artificial and oppressive ; but have they in ninety years been able to modify the people whom they crush into their moulds, and have they given them another nature ? Could we go back to the system of decentralization and small free associations ?

Perhaps there is a secret relation between the contradictions in Taine's work and the contrasts which one divines in his mind and character.

This logician is a poet. This abstractor has the most concrete style you can see. No writer has more continuously expressed himself by metaphors that are more coloured, or developed with more minuteness, or that are more exact down to the least detail. This commonly extends even as far as symbols and parables. And thus one fears that, the correctness of the images conquering in his mind the underlying truth, this suspicious positivist may have sometimes allowed himself to be deceived by words.

This man of violent and carnal imagination (you remember his studies of the Renaissance and of Flemish painting) has lived the life of an ascetic and a Benedictine. This great apostle of observation has lived in great retirement, and has associated little, I believe, with men of any other class than his own ; and this great collector of facts has sought them above all in books.

This determinist who regards history as a development of inevitable facts, and who has often artistically enjoyed the manifestations of force, has melted with compassion as soon as he saw blood and suffering near at hand. He would have been indulgent to Sulla and to Cæsar : Robespierre and Napoleon found him inexorable.

This enemy of the classic spirit has, in his need for unity, subdued reality to the most imperious simplifications and generalizations. His philosophy is to be found, in dramatized form, in the naturalist novel; and we know that the naturalist novel horrified him.

Through having seen too much of human beastliness in history, he ended by being afraid of men. In his later years his sympathy was evident for doctrines of which his own were the radical negation, and even for virtues which his own philosophy was most calculated to discourage.

This man of such uncompromising audacity of thought had become an energetic 'conservative.' (Was he one for the same frightful reason as Hobbes? We do not know.) And not only did he refuse the civil burial which alone would have been sincere, but he did not allow himself to be buried simply according to the rites of the religion into which he was born, rites which would have had, under the circumstances, but slight significance; he demanded—or accepted—a Protestant funeral. I never felt a greater intellectual melancholy than at that lying ceremony.

But this has not abolished his written work. Hippolyte Taine was one of our masters. The positivist period of our literature—that which begins about 1855 and which we see ending—bears the profound traces of his imprint.

One only discovers new truths by means of great foregone conclusions which bring with them quite as many errors. What does it matter ? The truths remain. Taine is the writer who has most strongly made us feel and understand the animal and the machine that man always is. Only that is a truth of which we have seen enough, and truths a little different are beginning to attract us more. And then it will happen with Taine as with other great inventors or rejuvenators of ideas; men will abandon him for thirty years—to return again to him.

GEORGE SAND

THE Porte Saint-Martin theatre is going to
revive that delicious romantic comedy, *Les
Beaux Messieurs de Bois-Doré* ; and the Odéon
promises to give us *Claudie,* that rustic drama
whose first act, at least, is a masterpiece, a
moving and grandiose Georgic. I am pleased
at this—just as I was pleased last month
when I noticed the beginning of a return of
minds and hearts towards Lamartine. For
in proportion as this century advances sadly
towards its end, I feel in myself more love for
those ample, magnificent, and fruitful geniuses
who gave lustre to its first fifty years.

You know how little resemblance there is
between the two halves of the seventeenth
century, and how literature, heroic and romantic with d'Urfé, Corneille, and the great
Blue-Stockings, returned, about 1660, to
more truth with Racine, Molière, and Boileau.

But do you not find that, allowing for the difference of time, something similar has taken place in our own century?

After the glorious reign of generous and believing optimist and idealist writers, who loved dreams, there has taken place a movement towards a literature that is realist, very gloomy, and very stern. The catastrophe of 1870 also came to increase the gloom and bitterness of people's feelings. The great confident and expansive souls who deluged our grandfathers with poetry and imaginings seemed to be very ingenuous to their grandchildren, and these latter had become almost indifferent to them. I remember that when I was younger I intoxicated myself as much as anybody with the heavy wine of naturalism (so ill-named). And it must be admitted that in spite of excesses and misunderstandings, this return to the truth has not been unfruitful, and that, moreover, this reaction was inevitable and in perfect conformity with the most assured laws of literary history.

But it seems that this movement is already very nearly exhausted. People are beginning to be very tired both with the documented novel and with the artistic and neurotic style of writing. And this is why they are returning to the neglected gods, and why these are going to become dear and beneficent to us.

And why not return to the love of George Sand ? She is, perhaps, along with Lamartine and Michelet, the soul that has most broadly reflected and expressed the thoughts, the hopes, and the loves of the first half of this century. The woman in her was good and original ; and as for her work, part of it will be beautiful eternally, and the rest has remained most interesting to the historian of minds.

I

There was, in George Sand, together with an ardent imagination and a great power of loving, a sound and robust temperament and a foundation of good sense which always came back to itself. She had, in an eminent degree, all the virtues of an honourable man. It was also said that she loved like a man— without more scruples, and in the same way.

Do not believe it. Only she was of a generous nature, capable of much action and much feeling ; her blood flowed warmly and abundantly in her veins like that of an ancient goddess or of a fawness who dwelt in the sacred woods. Therefore she loved with transport. But each time she felt herself called back by the imperious duty of her literary vocation ; and those interruptions brought it about that she loved often and did not seem to love long. She could neither keep herself from passion nor adhere to it, her true inclination being to pity and maternal tenderness.

The liberties of her life were in many cases only deviations, perhaps excusable, due to her goodness. She was a lover only in order that she might be a better friend, and her destiny was to be the friend of many.

In all this there was nothing of masculine debauchery, which is essentially egotistic and cares nothing for its associates. Add that this magnanimous woman's adventures of the heart could be explained by her romantic feeling, by the gift which she had of seeing creatures more beautiful and more lovable than they are. She followed nature, as they used to say in the last century, and her faculty

for idealizing furnished her with opportunities
for following it often. Many of my dearest
contemporaries do far worse, I assure you.
Their mania for analysis, their fear of being
dupes, and perhaps an impoverishment of
their blood have made them incapable of
loving, and have reduced them to an unwholesome search for rare sensations. There is
not the least trace of neurosis in George Sand.
There was always health in her sentimental
errors.

II

Her work has been blamed as romantic ;
and the fact is that it was very much so, and
in two ways—in its action and characters,
and in its ideas.

The first of these does not offend me, and
even amuses me. For, in the first place, in
her it is absolutely spontaneous ; it flows
from her without an effort. She has an
imagination which, naturally and by an irresistible need, transforms and embellishes reality,
and finds combinations of charming and unexpected facts. She was born a minstrel, so to
speak, and a teller of tales. She remained

to the end the little girl who in the Berry hedgerows invented stories to amuse the little shepherds. I am sure that the strange and mysterious adventures of *L'Homme de Neige*, of *Consuelo*, and of *Flamarande* would still delight me. And what luxuriant fantasy, what an agreeably poetic vision of things there are in *Les Beaux Messieurs de Bois-Doré*, *Le Château des Désertes*, or *Teverino* !

As for the characters, I know well that in her early novels one meets rather too many Renés in petticoats, grandsons of Saint-Preux, workmen poets and philosophers, great ladies in love with peasants—and that all of them declaim a good deal. But, first of all, they all declaim naturally, as one breathes. Then, as time passes, these characters become less unpleasing. As they are not our contemporaries, their falseness no longer bothers us. We see in them only evidences of the romanticism of an epoch ; and we even end by liking them because they pleased our fathers.

As for the other element of her romanticism, that of ideas—well ! it does not offend me either. The magnificent and vague mysticism of *Spiridion* or *Consuelo*, the rather incoherent but truly evangelical Socialism of *La Péché de Monsieur Antoine* or of *Le Meunier d'Angibaut*, her faith in progress, her humanitarianism—all this pleases one in this excellent woman with the Arcadian imagination, because in her, to repeat it once more, all comes from the heart and gushes out from it in large waves. Her philosophical and socialistic romanticism is also, rightly understood, one of the forms of her goodness. To believe to this extent in the future reign of justice, is to be good towards the universe, is to pardon reality for being at present so very mixed.

If this romanticism has fallen into disfavour for some time past, the reason is that we are very miserable beings. The dream displeased us, not because it made us feel the real more keenly, but because it was merely.a dream. It was, as it were, a depravation of our intelligence. We took pleasure in the sight of the evil world from a strange disease of pride ; we preferred the world to be ugly in order that we might appear strong when we saw that it was ugly and said so. In our obstinacy to regard and depict the evil, there was a refusal of what was better, an evil sentiment that seemed to come from the devil. We did not desire to embellish life by hopes and dreams, so proud were we of finding it ignoble, and so much did this easy pessimism absolve us in our own eyes from everything.

Let us turn, it is time to do so, towards that land of Utopia so dear to George Sand. She has reflected in her books all the imaginings of her time ; and, as she was a woman, she has added to her own dream those of all the men whom she has loved. This part of her work, which used to seem faded and time-worn, attracts me to-day as much as the rest. The world lives only by dreams.

III

For . what is George Sand still blamed ? Pharisees have said that her first novels ruined many young women, and—what an exquisite jest !—the naturalist novelists have spoken like the Pharisees. M. Zola shows us clumsily in *Pot-Bouille* a little middle-class woman who falls through having read *André*.

233

Alas ! Those who could fall after having read *André* or *Indiana* were ripe for the fall ; and perhaps without *Indiana* they might have fallen lower and more brutally. If, in her first novels, George Sand appeared to admit the absolute right of passion, it was solely of that passion which is ' stronger than death ' and which causes death to be desired or despised. It is possible that her novels, badly understood, may have counted for something in Madame Bovary's errors, but then it was thanks to them that there remained in her enough nobleness of soul to seek a refuge in death. Without them, Emma would not have had the frankness to wish to run away with Rodolphe, and she would have accepted the money from the notary, Tuvache. Our neurasthenics would find great moral profit in reading *Jacques* or *Lélia*.

IV

However, if George Sand's romanticism continues to displease you, you will find in her masterpieces enough truth, and much more than has been said. Selected truth, as truth always is when expressed in a work of art. Only the selection in them is made in a direction contrary to that which has prevailed during the past twenty years.

I do not speak of her charming young girls ; and I do not remind you that she has made subtle and powerful analyses of the character of artists and actors (*Horace, Le Beau Laurence*, etc.). But it should not be forgotten that George Sand invented the novel of rural life. She was the first, I believe, who truly understood and loved the peasant, the man who lives far away from Paris, in the provinces where originality of manners has been preserved. She was the first who felt what was grand and poetical in his simplicity, in his patience, in his communion with the Earth ; she enjoyed the archaisms, the slownesses, the metaphors, and the savour of his coloured language ; she was struck by the depth and calm tenacity of his feelings and his passions ; she showed him in love with the soil, greedy for work and for gain, prudent, distrustful, but of strong sense, very fond of justice, and open to the mysterious.

What we also owe to George Sand is almost a renewal (by force of sincerity) of the feeling for nature. She knew it better, she was more familiar with it, than any of those among her predecessors who have described landscapes. She truly lived the life of the earth, and without setting herself to do so. She was the most natural, the least laboured, the least studied of the writers who described landscapes. Unlike others who must frequently see nature from above and arrange it or lend it their own feelings, she delivered herself up to the charms of things and allowed them to penetrate her intimately. Without any doubt she has taught us to love with a more abandoned tenderness the beneficent and divine Nature who brings to her faithful ones appeasement, serenity, and goodness.

Goodness is one of the words that return frequently to her. Another word, quite near it, is that of fecundity, happy abundance. She poured out her narratives in a regular stream, like an inexhaustible spring—but almost without plan or design, scarcely knowing better where she went than does a large fountain in the great woods. Her very style, ample, easy, fresh, and full, does not recommend itself either by its subtlety or its extraordinary brilliancy, but by qualities which also seem to spring from goodness and to be related to it.

George Sand has been the womb which received, in somewhat confused order, the most generous ideas. She has been a nursing mother who poured poetry and fine stories over men. She is the Isis of the contemporary novel, the ' good goddess ' with the multiple breasts which are always flowing. It is good to refresh oneself in that stream of milk.

' THE whole succession of men,' says Pascal,
' during the course of so many centuries,
ought to be considered as the same man who
exists always and who learns continually.'
Now it is tiresome to be always learning.
Experience imparts wisdom, but it does not
gladden much. Just as a man who has
passed mature age, full of memories, of knowledge, and of melancholy, goes back over the
course of the years, recalls his childhood and his
youth, and takes pleasure in living them over
again, telling himself that they were the best
thing he has had, so humanity, having reached
the age of history and criticism, oppressed by its
own experience, weary of carrying in its skull
all the knowledge accumulated by the ages, yet
finds in its own antiquity resources against the
boredom of continuance, and takes pleasure
in picturing to itself the different states of
mind and conscience through which it has

formerly passed. Even criticism, which so often saddens it, endeavours to contrive for it those resurrections which amuse it. And criticism is aided in this by a sort of obscure memory of the times in which we were not yet alive, and the aptitude for imagining them. As our bodies, before seeing the light, passed successively through all the stages of life, beginning with that of the molluscs, and still contain the elements of those incomplete organizations which they have left behind, so the modern soul seems made up of several souls, contains, so to speak, those of gone centuries, and we seize again in ourselves, when we wish to make the effort, an Aryan, a Celt, a Greek, a Roman, a man of the Middle Ages.

For example, Rousseau and his school made themselves again into primitive men and ' savages.' The men of the Revolution revived the early days of the Roman Republic. Of the exactness of those internal resurrections, I shall say nothing now. The poets of the Pleiad believed that they sang in Greece, at the festivals of Bacchus, or beside the Tiber, under Horace's vine-tree. To-day criticism renders this sort of intercourse easier and

239

more attractive to us. All epochs, better known and reconstituted in their proper colours, attract us in turn, and we live in them with all our human ancestors.

Above all, we love to live with the Greeks, and we take pleasure in saying that they are our true intellectual fathers, and that we resemble them. It is the Hellenic soul that many artists and writers of our days have preferred to awaken in themselves and in their works. The religion of the Greeks appears to them the finest ; their life, the most natural and the noblest ; their art, the most perfect. André Chénier begins our initiation into the mysteries of pure beauty and accomplished form ; Cymodocæa is almost the only grace in Chateaubriand's *Martyrs* ; Béranger himself had his Greek dream :—

> ' Oui, je fus Grec ; Pythagore a raison.' [1]

And Musset :—

> ' Grèce, ô mère des arts, . . .
> Je suis un citoyen de tes siècles antiques ;
> Mon âme avec l'abeille erre dans tes portiques.' [2]

---

[1] ' Yes, I was a Greek, Pythagoras is right.'

[2] ' Greece, O mother of the arts. . . . I am a citizen of thy antique ages ; my soul flits with the bee about thy porticos.'

Hugo several times in the *Légende des Siècles* applies his lips of bronze, his prophet's lips, to the flute of Sicily. Théophile Gautier, Paul de Saint-Victor, M. Cherbuliez, and many others cannot console themselves for the death of the fair Gods of Greece ; Heine discovers the island to which they have been relegated ; M. Théodore de Banville makes them pass into the studio of Paul Veronese. Their cult goes on increasing. The latest poets, MM. Leconte de Lisle, Sully Prud-homme, Louis Ménard, France, Sylvestre, are in love with them. Politicians speak of the Athenian Republic as if they knew what they were talking about. When M. Taine dis-cusses Greek art, one feels, beneath the solidly clamped deductions and beneath that poet-logician's brilliant style, a heart that melts in tenderness, and M. Renan, at the Acropolis, addresses his moving prayer to Pallas Athene. In proportion as democracy, as what is called the inelegant, ascends, deli-cate souls turn with the more adoration to-wards the country and towards the ages of irreproachable beauty and of harmonious life. As Ronsard and his friends formerly sacri-

ficed with pomp a he-goat to Iacchos, several
of our contemporaries could willingly offer
to some statue of Venus rising from the foam
or Venus victorious, not a heifer or a lamb, but
fruits, milk, and wine, singing the while verses
of Leconte de Lisle to an air by Massenet.

I

No one has seized upon this Greek dream
with more fervour, nurtured it with more predilection, expressed it with more enthusiasm ;
no one has better restored and attached to this
antique dream even the most modern thoughts
and feelings ; no one has better given to this
artistic piety the appearance of a moral cult
and of a faith that rules over life ; no one
has mingled more joyously in the procession
of the Pan-Athenians than Madame Juliette
Lamber. Her least disputable originality is
the very ardour of her Pagan faith.

Her work is almost entirely an apotheosis
of the earth and of life upon the earth. Passionate belief in the goodness of things ; intoxication of being and feeling ; free life
which is none the less noble for being happy ;
obedience to the natural inclinations rendered

inoffensive by a fondness for measure, by a studious adoration of beauty ; reconciliation of matter and spirit ; harmonious development of the complete man, the exercise of his superior faculties sufficing to temper and purify the instincts of the flesh—that is the basis of her novels.

' What am I ? I am a Pagan. That is what distinguishes me from other women.'[1]

But it is not only because Greek religion and life, as she imagines them, seem beautiful to her, that Madame Juliette Lamber embraces them so ardently. She believes that a well-endowed nature, if it is allowed to develop freely, takes this direction of its own accord. Our misfortune is that, from our childhood, there are impressed upon us ideas, beliefs, and anxieties about the other world by which our nature is falsified for ever ; for we never free ourselves from those terrors, or at least some portion of them always remains. Then, in addition to the education which we receive, we submit in spite of ourselves more or less to the spirit of eighty generations which have all had this bent of

[1] *Païenne.*

tormenting themselves about another life, and of placing their ideal outside the terrestrial life.

' It is necessary to know what one sees, to feel only what one experiences. The sole lessons that my childhood experienced were such as ought to guard me from any religious notion.'

' My youth, I lived it in myself, by myself, without being constrained to live it in the youth of a hundred races, in the errors and decrepitudes of a hundred societies that are dead of old age.'

The way to restore its native virginity to our being, to secure for it the integrity of its youth, is to live in nature, to love her, to understand her, to have communion with her. One of Madame Juliette Lamber's most eminent merits is her passion for fine landscapes and her power to describe them. Her pictures are brilliant and grandiosely picturesque. They are the warm and luminous landscapes of the South ; and they are living, really filled with gods, nature having in them forms that are vaguely animal and that breathe : *mens agitat molem*.

' The ravaged sides of Luberon display entrails of gold. The summits of its hills assume the wrinkled aspects of the skin of mastodons. One of the summits has the form of a monster. He seems to swim on the waves of the earth, to stoop and rise in the rolling movements of the globe, whilst the flaky clouds, resting on the monster, surround him with driven foam.'

The author of *Païenne* feels with a rare violence the intoxication of forms, of light, of colours. There is in her Mélissandre, though she is so refined, something of the large animal and divine life of Maurice de Guérin's Centaur.

'I intoxicated myself by breathing the flame of the immortal star, I sought out its embraces ; I believed that I found a being similar to myself, more ardent, whom I endowed with an aureole, whom I personified, whose habits I shared, rising and going to bed when it did, in love with its glittering face, in despair at its disappearances as at the absence of an adored being. The sun was my first passion, my first worship.

' I gave animal shapes to the great forms of the mountains ; I found in them mysterious figures. When I rode at their feet I imagined to myself that I was dragging them with me in vertiginous races to the gallop of my horse. The trees accompanied me in a long file or in troupes ; I felt myself swept away by the movement of the whole earth beneath the gaze of all the stars ! Ah ! what fine rides are those with entire nature ! . . .'

In truth the demi-gods and the goddesses live in these deified landscapes. Madame Juliette Lamber's heroes and heroines have physical beauty, wealth, pride, courage, intelligence, spirit, genius. You will not here find secret sacrifices, anæmic melancholies, stifled passions (except, at least, in the first part of the story of Hélène). They are neither disgusted with life nor ashamed of love. They are superb and lyrical creatures whom one imagines to be like the lords and ladies who burst forth from those wonderful skies in the pictures and ceilings of the Italian Renaissance. It is of Veronese's canvases that they make us think, bear this in mind, far more than of the sober figures of the Panathenæa.

Their stories are extraordinary and simple. Hélène, disfigured by a malady, is dying because she is ugly and is not loved by that fine painter Guy Romain, her comrade and her husband. After an unsuccessful attempt to commit suicide, a fresh malady restores her beauty to her and gives her Guy's love. —Ida exiled from Crete, prefers her country and her gods to her weak lover, the Cypriote, who dies crushed by the marble statue of his rival, Apollo.—As for *Païenne*, it is merely a long and burning love duet, without a story or external incidents, and even without an interior drama ; for the lovers have hardly an hour's doubt, and pass their time making delightful discoveries in themselves or in one another. (It needed audacity and a certain passionate candour to conceive and undertake a book of this sort.)

Thus Madame Juliette Lamber's work is but the triumphant hymn of the most noble and joyous human feelings : the love of man and woman (*Païenne*), the love of country (*Grecque*), the love of beauty (*Laide*), and everywhere the love of nature, and the worship of the Greek gods ; for all are Pagans, and the Greek Ida is a practising Pagan. And Madame Juliette Lamber's patriotism strives also to be antique and Pagan. The motherland is a concrete thing : it is the sum of benefits that form for a people the sweetness and beauty of life ; here also mysticism is out of place. Lieutenant Pascal ends by recognizing that his ascetic patriotism, the worship of an abstraction to which he sacrifices his natural feelings, is but a sublime error, and he decides to love France in the person of a Frenchwoman.

This naturalism finds expression not only in Madame Juliette Lamber's frankly Pagan works, but in her shortest tales. All through them nature is more than loved—she is adored, and all through them the Greek divinities are evoked and invoked, even in dialogues between persons who have such middle-class names as Renaux or Durand. I do not pretend that this naturalism makes the conversations very natural; but it is enough that the author writes naturally in this way. Moreover, she loves and describes only the

landscapes of the south, the Provençal landscapes so similar to the sites of Greece. She
does not conceal her prejudice against Northern nature, against the nature of the land
of fir-trees, the nurse of mystic dreams,
of anti-human sentiments, of vague imaginings and austere morals. Love displays itself freely beneath the sun which encourages
it. The brothers, with the simplicity of demi-
gods, interest themselves and interpose in the
love affairs of their sisters. In this happy
world Juliet and Romeo do not die, and they
reconcile the Montagues and the Capulets.
And if a hermit is to be found at Saint-
Baume, he is a hermit of nature.

Naturalism, Paganism, neo-Hellenism, all
these words are equally fitting to designate
the spirit of Madame Juliette Lamber's books
—floating words, difficult to define. This
warns us that it is not precisely a question of
a philosophical system, of a theory of the
universe and of life, but rather of an intellectual and sentimental state. One would perhaps find, by looking at it closely, that at
bottom it is only a fantasy of the moderns
adorned with an ancient name ; one would

disentangle the portion of illusion, voluntary or not, which neo-Hellenism contains ; lastly, one would recognize to what an extent this fantasy is aristocratic, and how few persons are capable of it, but also how beautiful and beneficent it is.

II

We must waive the question whether, as Madame Juliette Lamber appears to believe, a well-endowed personality of our time and our race, abandoned to itself and withdrawn from all modern influences, would surely arrive at thinking, feeling, and living like an ancient Greek ; in other words, whether Greek life as a whole presents the most natural development of that rational animal, man.

We are brought up in a way different from Mélissandre, and our neo-Hellenism is rather something acquired than the fruit of nature. It consists in loving and admiring the art, religion, and literature of the Greeks (which implies a fair amount of study), and in endeavouring to give oneself the soul and life of an Athenian of the time of Pericles (some people would say, of an Ionian of the time of Homer).

It is clear, in the first place, that those who form this dream know that it is only a dream. We cannot suppress the twenty-five or thirty centuries which we inherit. We have within us germs deposited by the generations, that are not Greek and that we cannot stifle. We live in an environment which warns us that we are not Greeks, and which continually modifies us in one sense or another.

But this is not all. Is what we imagine under the name of Hellenism so very Greek? Is not neo-Hellenism newer than Greek? Do we represent Greek life to ourselves as it really was? Do we not love in it many things which we ourselves have put into it? Is there not, even in our admiration for Greek art, a share of noble and happy deception?

One says to us:

> ' Bien heureuse la destinée
> D'un enfant grec du monde ancien!' [1]

Another:

> ' Jadis j'aurais vécu dans les cités antiques . . .' [2]

---

[1] ' Happy the destiny of a Greek child of the ancient world!' (Sully-Prudhomme: *Croquis Italiens*.)

[2] ' Formerly I should have lived in the ancient cities,' etc. (Emmanuel des Essarts.)

They all tell us that they would like to have lived in Athens, there to have practised gymnastics, to have listened to the orators, to have joined in the processions, to have been present at the tragic performances which lasted entire days. Well, I would not ! I say so frankly. Perhaps it is implied that, when transported to Athens, we should there assume the heart and head of an Athenian ; but then we should no longer be ourselves. But suppose that we, such as we are, found ourselves transported to the resuscitated city of Pallas Athene, and compelled to live the life of its citizens ; do you think you would be very comfortable there ? Too many things would be missing—hearth and home, luxury, comfort, the intimacy of life and all the pleasures derived from the position of women in modern society : courtesy, politeness, and certain ideas and delicacies. It would be necessary always to live outside, always in the street or in a public place, always to be judging and voting, always to be occupied with politics, and yet have no real work to do. And we should have little freedom to think as we wished, witness Socrates, and we should be exposed, too, to the sorrow of being present at human sacrifices (they were performed at Salamis). These little annoyances would be compensated for, I shall be told, by the pleasure of living only with intellectual men, all handsome, all connoisseurs, all artists. ' There was once,' says M. Renan, ' a people of aristocrats, a public entirely composed of connoisseurs, a democracy which seized upon *nuances* of art so subtle that refined persons in our time scarcely perceive them.' M. Renan, who doubts so many things, has the air of not doubting this. Yet Thucydides and the orators sometimes give me a singular idea of this perfectly harmonious and intelligent life, and it seems to me that three-quarters of the jests of Aristophanes could only be addressed to rather coarse men. No, decidedly, it is better to live in the nineteenth century, in Paris if possible, or even in some pretty corner of the provinces.

Perhaps there is also some affectation and some deception in the admiration which many people display for Greek art. It becomes a superstition which they keep up and with which they please themselves, as if this alone placed them above the vulgar ; an exclusive religion which drives them to despise everything else. Look at how the Renaissance is treated by the sculptor Martial :

> ' It was the little artists of the Renaissance who invented the abstraction of impalpable things, the idea of the infused idea, the reflection of an indefinite sentiment of the indefinable.'[1]

And elsewhere :

> ' It seems to me that what I call the intimate, interior, domestic school is going to disappear. . . . Enough shadows, enough half-lights, enough Northern skies have been painted during the last three centuries, to speak only of painting. Already the young School, all that carries the future in its bosom, is turning towards the East, towards the lands of the warm sun, all of whose roads by land and sea lead to Greece.'[2]

They have in their mouths nothing but measure, sobriety, clearness, harmony, purity of lines, proportion, and they comment abundantly on the φιλοκαλοῦμεν μετ' εὐτελείας. I

[1] *Laide*, p. 17.   [2] *Laide*, p. 101.

am afraid, in truth, that they are less in love with Greek art than with the idea they form of it. One can say, in the first place, that they love that art only in a roundabout way, and because they are acquainted with another which is more complex and living, and which it pleases them to hold cheaply either out of satiety and lassitude or in order to show that they can detach themselves from it and that they are still superior to it. The very definitions which they give of Greek art imply the notion of something that goes beyond them. I am going to utter a blasphemy. Of course I love the serenity of the whole and a certain science of grouping in the friezes of the Parthenon ; but, try as I may, I see that everything is simplified to excess, that the young girls are too short, that such and such a figure is awkward and clumsy, etc. I know that people can see with other eyes, and can turn all this into a merit ; but I have in my mind and I know examples of an art which satisfies me far more. In order to say that Greek sculpture is what is supremely beautiful, it is necessary first of all to frame our definition of the beautiful for that express purpose. And, further, what makes us love this very simple art are reasons that do not belong to it, that come to us from our experience of a more tortured art, of a richer literature, and of a more refined sensibility.

And this is why, after having said of the Acropolis : ' That is a place where perfection exists ; there are not two of the species : this is it. . . . It was the ideal crystallized in Pentelican marble which showed herself to me ; ' after having sung the blue-eyed goddess (with what bewitching grace !) the enchanter Renan, in a diabolic palinode, gives Pallas Athene to understand that there is, however, something else in the world besides Greece, and that to be antique is to be old.

' I shall go further, orthodox goddess ; I shall tell you of the intimate depravation of my heart. Reason and good sense are not enough. There is poetry in frozen Strymon and in the intoxication of Thrace. Ages will come in which thy disciples will be regarded as the disciples of dullness. The world is larger than thou thinkest. If thou hadst seen the snows of the Pole and the

mysteries of the austral sky, thy brow,
O goddess who art always calm, would
not be so serene ; thy head, of greater
breadth, would comprehend divers forms
of beauty.'

III

One way of arranging everything is to enlarge Athene's brow, to give to modern ideas
and feelings something of the antique form.
Our artists have not failed to do this. To
mention only Madame Juliette Lamber's
novels, how many things are there in her
Hellenism that are not entirely Greek !

As far as I can judge, the ancient Greeks
may have been religious but they were not
devout ; they did not know what theologians
call affective piety. They conceived of prayer
either as a give-and-take commercial operation, or as a philosophical speculation. It
does not seem to me that there is the tone of
piety even in the hymn of Cleanthes to Jupiter, in the invocation of Lucretius to Venus,
or in the prayers that may be collected from
Seneca or Cicero, or in the tragic choruses.
I hardly see anything except the Bacchantes
and Hippolytus of Euripides in which a little

of that tone is heard. But how much more
it vibrates in the Christian prayers ! Now,
Madame Juliette Lamber's heroines—Hélène
and Ida—pray to Apollo or Artemis somewhat
in the same manner as a nun prays to Jesus
or the Virgin, with outbursts of love, an
abandonment of self, hallucinations, an assurance of being loved and preferred by her God.

In the same way the characters of these
Pagan novels bring to the love of nature a
violent and vague sensibility which the ancient Greeks do not seem to have known.
Most certainly the Athenians did not enjoy
the country as we do. Most of them lived
little in the fields, were pure citizens attached
to the pavements of the Pnyx or of the
Agora. As for their poets, some of them
certainly love and describe nature ; but
their landscapes are always short and simple,
even those of Theocritus ; there is scarcely
a touch of elaboration except in Bion and
some of the poets of the *Anthology*. Never
are there to be found in them any curiosities
of analysis, any efforts to express rare effects
of light and colour. Then their descriptions are always tranquil : they do not experi-

ence, before the spectacles of nature, the restless pleasure, the love-sickness of some moderns, and that species of voluntary intoxication which makes the heart throb a little. They enjoy the country, but they have no passion for it. There are, moreover, certain wild and formidable landscapes which delight us, but which would have been distinctly displeasing to them. They liked confined views, strictly limited and well constructed. They did not fall into transports before extraordinary pictures. A Greek would have been colder than Jean Lalande in the presence of a mass of orchids [1] ; a Greek would not have undertaken to analyse and to express in words the prodigious gamut of colours, the phantasmagoria of Lake Gardo at sunset ; [2] a Greek on a mountain would not have noted, or perhaps felt, an impression like this :

'Loftier summits rear themselves upwards. . . . One finds oneself suddenly alone in spaces where the eye has no longer more than a dazzling and radiant vision, where the expanded intelligence

[1] In *Jean et Pascal.*　　　　[2] *Jean et Pascal.*

becomes vague and has only perceptions of size, of light, of an immense circle.' [1]

Above all, a Greek would not have written, and would not have perfectly understood, passages like this :

' Hélène admires the universe and believes that she comprehends it. Yet, beneath what she sees, it seems to her that an unknown something attracts and beguiles her. What is this mystery of the real ? Where is it hidden ? In matter or in being ? Are the secrets of appearances written on what manifests itself to the eyes, or are they shut up in the depths within us ? ' [2]

Do not these words, which are doubtless not vain, answer to ill-defined and hardly definable feelings ? In truth, what does to love nature and ' comprehend ' her mean ? It means, in the first place, that she refreshes our blood, caresses our ears, amuses our eyes, and that she procures us an uninterrupted series of agreeable and buoyant sensations, which occupy us without troubling us, which move us not too deeply, which never weary

[1] *Païenne.*　　　　　　[2] *Laide.*

us, which repose and console, if you will,
from the labour of thought. Living in the
country, we take pleasure in the images it
offers us of a simpler life than ours, a life
which glides by degrees into unconscious life,
a life of animals, a life of trees and flowers,
a life of waters and clouds. The serenity of
this impersonal, and, in a sense, divine life
communicates itself to us by a sort of anima-
tion. Or, on the contrary, the unbridling
of the natural forces pleases the 'thinking
reed,' either through the reason, as Pascal
says, or through the beauty that it discovers
in the horror of their display. A painter has
other motives for loving nature ; he searches
in her for combinations of colours and lines
that art would not invent by itself. Another
thing also : we seize upon analogies between
our own life and that of nature, and, in applying them to ourselves, we taste the calm joy
of feeling our existence unrolling itself in
parallel lines with hers. She suggests to us
innumerable images, metaphors, and comparisons ; she furnishes us with symbols of
death and resurrection, of purification and a
second life. The Eleusinian Mysteries were

but the dramatic setting and celebration of those symbols. Then the infinity and eternity of nature, the immutability of her laws, whose fulfilment we can see continually around us in the smallest objects, all this teaches us wisdom, peace, and resignation when we feel ourselves so negligible a portion of this unbounded whole. Are these all the ways of being moved in the face of nature ? Perhaps there is another, at once more obscure and more violent. It is possible that the spectacle of nature and her fatal manifestations may arouse within us, I do not know how, the innate suffering that comes from feeling that we are finite, that we are but ourselves, and a vague desire to go out of ourselves and mingle with universal being. This is the supreme prayer of Saint Antony, the culmination of the temptation : ' I would like to descend to the depths of matter, to be matter." [1]

That is all, I think ; and yet there are here many feelings of which one does not find a trace in the writings of the ancients. But when the Pagan Mélissandre writes these mysterious phrases :

[1] Flaubert : *La Tentation de Saint Antoine.*

' I wished to know the secret of things. . . . My ideas were simple. They gravitated without effort towards the higher paths where one meets the gods. . . . I did not see them with my eyes alone, but with my whole being. . . . I penetrated the secret of the laws of exchange with nature, and mingled my individualtiy with the great whole. . . . I discovered the divine, human, and natural affinities of all force, all life. . . .'[1] one is not very sure that one understands this. One asks oneself what are those ' laws of exchange ' and those ' affinities.' Madame Juliette Lamber, I think in *Jean et Pascal*, gives an example of them which explains her thought. It is the oak, robust, welcoming, and gay, that has made the Gaul ; it is the fir-tree, stiff, prickly, and bad, that has made the German. These are curious but very arbitrary imaginings. A forest of fir-trees, with the solemnity of its colonnades and the bluish fairy-like effect of the bottom of its foliage, is as beautiful and can pour into the soul as noble thoughts as a forest of oaks.

[1] *Païenne.*

263

Besides, in ancient Gaul perhaps there were not more oaks than fir-trees.

' To comprehend nature ' is either what I have said just now, or it is simply to know botany and natural history. But the vague, pious, and contradictory Pantheism of Mélissandre is quite a different thing. There is in it a need of adoration, of communication with a divine person, the accumulated mysticism of fifty generations, which, not wishing to resort to the God of a positive religion, pours itself out over the universe, endows it with a benevolent soul, erects nature into a secret divinity which speaks to her elect, teaches them, and wants to have them entirely her own. Tiburcius himself says to Mélissandre when she is too much captivated by this religion of nature : ' This singular ferocity would have made you, but for my love, the priestess of a creed which, like the Christians, would sacrifice human personality to divine love.' [1] One sees that, from the very confession of the author, this is not Greek, that it is even anti-Greek.

We can say the same about its love. ' You

---

[1] *Païenne.*

will find in it,' says Madame Juliette Lamber,
' a double current, mystic and sensual.' Now
the ancient Greeks had hardly any knowledge
of the ' mystic current ' in love. Romanticism and reverie in passion, the religious form
given to the cult of woman, devout absorption in her contemplation, Petrarchism—
there is not much of all this in the Greeks,
and nothing, I think, similar to the state of
Tiburcius before Mélissandre :

> ' I have really possessed the happiness
> of the immortals. I have seen love bare
> itself, purify itself, become a religion, a
> worship, and a prayer. For the first
> time I have experienced the delight of
> internal adoration.' [1]

One does not imagine Sappho speaking in
this way as she left Phaon's arms.

It would be easy, by going on with this
analysis, to point out the same deviations, the
same refinement, or the same embellishment
in all the feelings of Madame Juliette Lamber's neo-Greeks. For instance, you know
the ardent patriotism of the author of *Grecque*.
No more humanitarian Utopias : for long

[1] *Païenne.*

enough we have invited the other peoples to universal fraternity ; we know what these generosities cost ; we ought to love our native country with a narrow, exclusive love, to love it in the style of the ancients ! The patriotism of the Cretan Ida and of Pascal Mamert has the ardour, the jealousy, and the intolerance of a religion. But, in truth, they labour too hard at it. We try in vain : we wish henceforth to be patriots in the style of an Athenian, of a Spartan, or of a Roman of the Republic ; but since we wish it, we are not so naturally. One thing distinguishes us from the other peoples : we would prefer not to hate them. We conceive of hatred only as the reverse side of a duty, of justice, of pity, and of honour. And that is not our fault. To compare ourselves only with the Greeks dear to Madame Juliette Lamber, one does not love a country that has made the Revolution (a good work, it is too late, moreover, to doubt this), in the same way as one loves a little city in which nothing mitigates the right of the strongest, and which includes slavery among its institutions. Add that one no longer loves a country with thirty-five

millions of inhabitants in the same way as
one loves a State with ten thousand citizens.
One of our officers would fall in another
Thermopylæ with as much heroism as the
soldiers of Leonidas : I believe that perhaps he
would have, as he fell, thoughts that the
Spartans and even the Athenians did not
know ; that he would obey more ideal motives, and that, his interest being less visibly
bound to that of a country more extensive and
more complex, there would be in his devotion
less of instinctive fury, more will, more
resignation, and a higher disinterestedness.

In default of the feeling, is the form of
Madame Juliette Lamber's novels Greek ?
In our literature I know nothing truly Greek
except the idylls of André Chénier, and perhaps some pieces by Leconte de Lisle (*Glaucé,
Clytie, L'Enlèvement d'Hélène*). The novel,
Grecque, observes the greatest care for the
antique form, and presents an interesting attempt to adapt the Homeric style to a modern
narrative. But still it has a concern for what
is picturesque, an inclination to be long and
detailed in its descriptions, a feeling for
nature of which the fervour and the curiosity

are things of to-day. Then, however successful this sort of an imitation may be, if it is too prolonged it runs a risk of tiring by demanding too continuous an effort of ' the sympathetic imagination,' an effort easy enough to make when one applies it to an antique work *regarded as genuine*, less easy when it is a question of a game, of a skilful exercise in imitation. As for Madame Juliette Lamber's other novels, it has been seen well enough from quotations (for here the substance gets the better of the form) whether they have always the Greek tone. Even in those pages where the author is most careful, she writes in ' poetical prose '—that is to say, though in a more modern style, and with all the differences you will, in the tone of *Les Incas*, of *Atala*, and of *Les Martyrs*—and you know quite well that that prose is not too Greek.

IV

Thus everything escapes us, and it seems that, contrary to our anticipation, we were pursuing a shadow. We have found in none of the separate elements of Madame Juliette Lamber's work that Hellenism of which, however, those elements when united gave us the idea. At least, it has appeared to us so closely mingled with other ideas and other feelings that it was almost impossible to distinguish it clearly from them and to isolate it. Each passion, each impression, each phrase, one might say, is visibly three thousand years later than a verse of Homer, and is twenty-four centuries later than a verse of Sophocles, and shows to those who know how to look, as by an involuntary and indelible sign, the refinement of its epoch. What then is there Greek in the composition of this Paganism, and how does it happen that what is in none of the parts expresses itself (one cannot deny it) in the whole?

What still increases our embarrassment is that there is more than one way of understanding this word, Paganism. Listen to an anecdote. It was in a house where Théophile Gautier, M. Chenavard, and M. Louis Ménard, the author of *La Morale avant les Philosophes*, were together at dinner.

'What pleases me in Paganism,' Gautier had just said, ' is that it has no morality.'

'What! no morality?' said M. Chenavard. ' What of Socrates ?' What of Plato ? What of the philosophers ? '

' What ! the philosophers ? ' replied M. Ménard. ' It was they who corrupted the purity of Hellenic religion ! '

It is rather with M. Louis Ménard's feeling that Madame Juliette Lamber would range herself. ' I am a Pagan,' says Madeleine to her cousin from Venice, ' but the same reason that attaches you to the poetry of the primitive Church makes me only accept from Paganism the beliefs of the first ages of Greece.'[1]

And I believe that, in truth, it is M. Louis Ménard who is right, and also Théophile Gautier, properly understood. All this vague Paganism only assumes a somewhat clear meaning from opposition to Christianity, to the Christian conception of man and of life, to the spirit of Christian morality. Now, the essence of that morality, what is proper to it and distinguishes it from natural morality, is assuredly contempt for the body, hatred and terror of the flesh. La Bruyère has a remark that goes deep : ' The only crime known to the pious is incontinence.' The

[1] *Jean et Pascal.*

opposite feeling is eminently Pagan. In the language of the people, ' to live like a Pagan ' (and the phrase does not always imply serious reprobation, and is sometimes uttered with a smile), is simply not to follow the prescriptions of the Church and to trust oneself to the good natural law.

By taking Hellenism in the sense of Paganism, and Paganism in the sense of anti-Christianity, one ends then by coming to an understanding. Madame Juliette Lamber's Paganism is, at bottom, a passionate protest against what in the Christian belief is hostile to the body and the life of earth, what is anti-natural and supernatural in it, and, to be still more precise, against the dogma of original sin and its consequences :

> ' " You believe," says Madeleine, speaking of the Christian hermits, " in the poetry of men who detested nature, who only sought out her rudeness, her harshness, her intemperances, in order to have the right to curse her." ' [1]

And further on :

> ' " No, I have no Christian beliefs,

[1] *Jean et Pascal.*

Spedone, my noble cousin, not one !
And do you want my whole opinion ?
Woman ought to be the irreconcilable
enemy of Christianity. All the mistrust,
all the insults, all the hatreds of its doctrines are for her. Woman is the great
peril, the great temptation, the devil's
great tool, the great demon. Love,
which she inspires, is sin and evil !
Her beauty is a trial, her wit a snare,
her sensibility a sorcery. All the
enviable gifts of the generous, of the
poetical, of the artistic nature become in
Christianity evil gifts. Is it not so,
Jean ? "

' " You are right, you speak well,
Madeleine," I replied. " Christianity
gives to man contempt for the joys of
this world, and consequently alienates
him from woman, who is their dispenser.
It is logical in its mistrust. Woman is
closer to nature than man. She exercises a direct power from it in maternity.
Jesus turns away from nature and from
his mother with disdain. ' What is
there common between me and thee ? '

asks the Saviour of souls of them both. Nothing, Lord ! You deny your mother both by your birth and by your miracles. Jesus only imposes his hands on the great reality in order to trouble its laws, in order to overthrow the simple and determined attributes of things, in order to walk on the waters, in order to raise the dead. . . ." ' [1]

Thus, to true neo-Greeks, Christianity is the enemy and the foreigner. Hellenism was the tranquil development of the mind of the Aryan race : Christianity has been the perversion of this luminous genius by the sombre genius of the Semites. Thenceforward the frightful anxiety about the ' hereafter,' the subordination and sacrifice of this earthly life to the dream of another life, have blighted, lessened, and corrupted mankind. The extreme neo-Greeks even trace the evil as far back as Socrates, a false Hellene who was properly condemned to death for impiety. The absorption of the Semitic virus infected the West with a malady that lasted a thousand years, and it is yet hardly cured. The

[1] *Jean et Pascal.*

Middle Ages are the crime of Christendom, Michelet has shown this, etc.

It would, in my opinion, be a pity if history were as simple as this. But it is possible to say that things happened a little differently. I need not indicate all that may be opposed to it, though in these matters everything is almost equally probable and equally incapable of proof. But, in the first place, when one race undergoes the influence of another, there have been, apparently, secret tendencies towards this. It must be remarked, too, that Hellenism was at a very low ebb when Christianity appeared. It was, moreover, Greeks who formulated the Christian dogmas ; one could say that it was Greeks who altered the purity of primitive Christianity. And if one says that Gnosticism is not Greek, that it has an Oriental and Buddhist origin, in that case it was Aryans who lent it to Aryans. And if the barbarians of the West embraced Christianity with so much fervour, it was doubtless because it answered to some need of their gross and dreamy souls. And those barbarians were also Aryans, that is to say, brothers of the Greeks ; at least, unless we must resign ourselves to the loss of the antique unity of the race in the famous ' central plateau,' a unity that is now, it appears, greatly disputed.

But all this is only prattling ' about cabbages and kings.' The Middle Ages and Christianity could be defended in a more serious manner from the contempt and hatred of some neo-Greeks.

If we moderns have so quick a sensibility and a ' nervousness ' of which we are proud— sometimes a little prouder than is reasonable —the cause perhaps is because the men of the Middle Ages, whose blood flows in us, had violent passions of a nature different, at least so it would seem, griefs, aspirations, and intimate terrors different from those of the ancient Greeks. The Christian faith, by mingling with all human passions, complicated them and added to them the idea of the ' hereafter ' and the hope or fear of the things beyond the tomb. The thought of the other life changed the aspect of this life, called forth furious sacrifices, resignations of infinite tenderness, and mortal despairs. Madeleine was wrong to pity herself a moment ago : woman, become the great temptress and the devil's snare, has inspired desires and adorations all the more ardent, and has occupied quite another place in the world. The malediction hurled at the flesh has dramatized love. Fresh passions have come into existence—a paradoxical hatred of nature, the love of God, faith, contrition. By the side of a debauchery exasperated by the very fear of hell, there have been purity and chivalrous chastity ; by the side of the greatest wretchedness, and amidst blind ferocities, there has been a greater charity, a compassion for human destiny in which the whole heart has melted. There have been conflicts of instincts, of passions, of beliefs, internal struggles unknown before, a complication of the moral conscience, a deepening of sadness, and an enrichment of feeling. I should be sorry for my part to think that Saint Paul had died from his fall on the road to Damascus ; that the Empire, completely Hellenized, had little by little annexed the barbarians instead of being invaded by them, and that the philosophers of the second century had succeeded in extracting a universal religion from polytheism, and that it continued for two thousand years (all very unreasonable hypotheses) ; for I am as persuaded as one can be of anything, that the human soul would not be the rare and complete instrument that it is to-day. The field of our memories and of our impressions would be infinitely poorer. There are skilful combinations and delicate gradations of ideas and feelings of which we would be still ignorant. We would not have among us, I am afraid, exquisite personalities whom I could name, ' Epicureans with Christian imaginations ' like Chateaubriand, or pious sceptics and light-hearted pessimists like M. Renan.

No, no, the Middle Ages should not be cursed. It was through them that Pallas Athene's heart was softened and her brow enlarged so that ' to-day she comprehends several forms of beauty.' And it is the memory of the Middle Ages and their Christianity which gives at once its ardour and its artistic refinement to the Paganism of several of our contemporaries. If the whole Middle Ages had not wept and bled beneath the Cross, would Madame Juliette Lamber so thoroughly enjoy her Greek Gods ?

V

To sum up, Hellenism is for the men of to-day a dream of a natural and happy life, dominated by the love and quest of beauty which is above all plastic and freed from any ultra-terrestrial care. This dream is supposed, rightly or wrongly, to have been realized formerly by the Hellenes. Those of the time of Homer, or those of the time of Pericles ? There is no agreement on this point, but it is of little moment.

This dream perhaps implies an incomplete idea of human nature ; for the need of the supernatural and preoccupation with it are as natural to some men as their other feelings.

This dream supposes—in those for whom it is more than a passing fancy, and who in its favour forget or despise two thousand years which are not, however, without interest— an excessively optimistic conception of the world and of life. This dream lets it be understood that there are not on earth horrible physical sufferings, incurable infirmities, deaths of beloved children, monstrous injustice in the distribution of good and ill, sacrificed beings of whom one asks why they live, other perverse and evil beings, a blind, brutal, and miserable mass ; for the most intelligent and the best, frightful and unmerited pangs, and, in their absence, inevitable hours of sadness and the feeling of the uselessness of all things.

This dream, whatever else it may be, is the dream of a select few. It needs a fair acquaintance with literature. It does not seem destined ever to clothe itself in a precise form, or, above all, in a popular form. It is, in conformity with the persons to whom it appeals, an aristocratic amusement or faith. Stripped of the form which lettered persons give it and of the poetical reminiscences with which it is almost completely blended, and placed within reach of the people, it would either fade away or turn into a crude and rudimentary sensualism. And the grossest and even the most savage manner of understanding Christian dogma is preferable for the happiness and dignity of the simple.

This dream, if one wishes to express nothing save it alone, will produce distinguished works, but a little cold and only to be appreciated by a small number of the initiated.

But these are only extreme consequences, and we know that logic often errs. The exclusive cult of a single one of the forms of life would not perhaps suffice to fill our life, nor to fortify and console us in the hour of trial ; but in reality, a sympathy, a curiosity of this sort, is always accompanied, whether we know it or not, by other sympathies. We baptize with a name borrowed from the historical period which we prefer, not only what is best in the whole past life of humanity, but what we feel is best in ourselves and in the life of our own time. In this way, Hellenism is no longer more than a particular form of the great and salutary ' philosophy of curiosity.'

Thus understood, Hellenism is a fine dream, and can even serve in dark hours as a support for the moral life by the habits of serenity and pride which it engenders in its elect. It is not impossible that to those chosen souls love and beauty may be a sufficient director and consoler. Add that Hellenism has the advantage, considerable at the present moment, of saving its adepts from a pessimism which is perhaps true, but which is none

the less wrong, and which, moreover, is becoming disagreeable and vulgar. Finally,
when I spoke of the coldness of neo-Hellenism in literature, I was doubtless mistaken.
Read Madame Juliette Lamber's novels. One
feels so well a soul beneath the form, artificial and composite as that form sometimes
is, and, admitting that she desires to grasp
a mirage, she puts her whole heart so thoroughly into the pursuit, she torments herself so strangely in order to attain he Greek
serenity, her Hellenism—perhaps less pure
and less authentic than she believes—is so
completely her religion, her life, her all, that
one must admit that her work, in spite of
errors and of singularities and of all the
reasons why it should be cold, is yet warm
and living, and that it will remain at the very
least as a rare effort of ' sympathetic imagination ' in a time which prides itself greatly
on that imagination, and not without reason,
for one can live and be almost happy by its
means.

MADAME SARAH BERNHARDT

I

In ' Théodora '

The grace, the charm, the light, or rather the unwholesome and diabolic attraction of this Byzantine phantasmagoria is Madame Sarah Bernhardt. Who was it that said that her golden voice has been broken by singing every day, everywhere throughout both worlds ? It seemed to me to sound as deliciously as formerly. But have you noticed her strange elocution ? Why this continuous chanting ? What an odd notion it is for her to sing her phrases to a sort of funereal tune in order to show that it is the Empress who is speaking ! This official and Imperial elocution, so violently opposed to the usual way of speaking, is the height of convention. But does one care for this ? One is seduced, I tell you. In what way ?

If we tried to set out the causes of the powerful attraction which Madame Sarah Bernhardt exerts on a great number of us, I think that we should see that these are three. First of all, she is very intelligent, understands the parts she plays, constructs them carefully, and plays them without sparing herself. But let us pass on, for other artists possess these merits in the same degree. The second cause is her physical appearance and also the *timbre* of her voice. You know the immense share which physical gifts have in an actor's talent, or, if you wish, in the total effect he produces. Many nervous, capricious, and frivolous people —unless, indeed, they are, on the contrary, very philosophic—take account of nothing except the actor's personality, which is sympathetic or antipathetic to them, and that is all. They like or dislike people for such reasons as the length of their noses. But it is especially in the case of actresses that physical appearance is of extreme importance. Now heaven has endowed Madame Sarah Bernhardt with exceptional gifts : it has made her strange, surprisingly slender and supple, and it has covered her thin face with the disturbing grace of a Bohemian, a gipsy, a Tartar, a something which makes one think of Salome, of Salammbô, of the Queen of Sheba.

And Madame Sarah Eernhardt marvellously exploits this air of a princess in a story, of a fantastic and distant creature. She dresses and makes up delightfully. In the first act, lying on a bed, a mitre on her head and a big lily in her hand, she resembles the fantastic queens of Gustave Moreau, those dream figures, in turn hieratical and serpentine, possessing a mystical and sensual attraction. Even in modern parts she keeps this strangeness which is given her by her elegant thinness and her Oriental, Jewish type. And, in addition, she has her voice, which she knows how to turn to account with the happiest audacity—a voice which is a caress, and which seems to touch you like fingers—so pure, so tender, so harmonious, that Madame Sarah Bernhardt, disdaining to speak, one day began to chant, and that she has dared to employ perhaps the most artificial style of elocution that has ever been heard in a theatre. At first she chanted verses; now she chants prose. And her influence has not been negligible over the number of actors and actresses who also chant prose and verse, or who at least try to chant them ; for, you see, there is no one like her !

But the greatest originality of this entirely personal artist is that she does what no one had dared to do before her—she acts with her whole body. Mind you, this is unique. If the most emancipated of girls plays a lover's part, she does not deliver herself up to it entirely. She does not dare, and she cannot, for she is thinking of her part. She does not embrace and clasp in earnest, and she has relatively moderate conventions, which conventionally take the place of a warmer mimicry. The woman is on the stage, but it is not she who is acting, it is the actress. With Madame Sarah Bernhardt, on the contrary, it is the *woman* who is acting. She truly gives herself entirely up to it. She clasps, embraces, swoons, twists, dies, she envelops her lover with the windings of a snake. Even in scenes in which she expresses other passions than that of love, she is not afraid to display, if I may say so, what is most intimate, most secret, in her feminine person. That, I think, is the most astonishing novelty in her manner —she puts into her parts, not only all her soul, all her mind, and all her physical grace, but also all her sex. So bold a procedure would be offensive in others ; but nature having so moulded her, and having given her the aspect of a fantastic princess, her light and ideal grace saves all her audacities, and makes them exquisite.

I know well that there are also other elements in Madame Sarah Bernhardt's talent ; but it is not the talent which I have wished to express, it is the attraction, and be it understood that I only speak of it for those who feel it.

II

In ' Fédora '

The harmonious and pliant woman, the electric and fantastic woman has conquered Paris afresh. It resisted her for some time past, it even began to be unjust to her. And perhaps also she had but imperfectly succeeded in giving a soul to Marion, and had made Ophelia too distant, cold, and sing-song a creature. But with Fédora we have found again the real Sarah, the unique and all-powerful, she who does not content herself with chanting, but who lives and vibrates in her whole being. It is true that this part, like that of Théodora, has been made expressly for her, to her measure, and fitting her closely. Madame Sarah Bernhardt is eminently, by her character, her gait, and type of beauty, a Russian princess, at least if she is not a Byzantine Empress or a Begum of Muscat ; passionate and feline, gentle and violent, neuropathic, eccentric, enigmatic, woman-abyss, woman I know not what. Madame Sarah Bernhardt has always upon me the effect of a very strange person who returns from a great distance ; she gives me the sensation of exoticism, and I am thankful to her for reminding me that the world is large, and that it is not confined to the shadow of our own steeple, and that man is a various and multiple being, capable of everything. I love her for all which I feel is unknown within her. She could, without surprising me, enter into a convent of nuns of Saint Claire, discover the North Pole, have herself inoculated with the virus of hydrophobia, assassinate an emperor, or marry a negro king. She alone is more alive and more incomprehensible than a thousand other human creatures. Above all, she is as much of a Slav as it is possible to be ; she is much more of a Slav than all the Slavs I have ever met and who were often Slavs—in no respect whatsoever.

She has therefore played the part of Féodora marvellously. That part, which is all passion, happily forced her to vary her chanting and to break away from her hieratic attitudes. Her acting has again become mobile and poignant. In order to represent anguish, pain, despair, love, fury, she has found cries that moved our very souls because they came from the lowest depths of hers. Truly she gives herself up, abandons herself, lets herself completely loose, and I do not think it is possible to express the feminine passions with more intensity. But while her acting is terribly true, it remains deliciously poetical, and this is what distinguishes it from the vulgar panthers of melodrama. With her, those great explosions remain harmonious, obey a secret rhythm which corresponds with the rhythm of fine attitudes. Nobody poses, moves, bends, lengthens, glides, or falls like Madame Sarah Bernhardt. Her acting is at once elegant, sovereignly expressive, and unexpected. Look at it : all those successive silhouettes seem the visions of a refined and daring painter. That is hardly simple, but how ' amusing ' it is, in the sense in which the word is used in the studios ! Nobody dresses like her either, with a more lyrical sumptuousness, or a surer audacity. On that frail and elastic body, on that false thinness which in the theatre is an element of beauty, for owing to it attitudes are outlined with more clearness and decision, the contemporary manner of dressing, insensibly transformed, assumes a suppleness which one does not see in other women, and as it were the grace and dignity of historical costume. And the acting of this great artist is not only poignant and enveloping at the same time ; it is excessively personal and, so to speak, coloured. I have already remarked that, in some passages, nothing is more strangely conventional than Madame Sarah Bernhardt's elocution. Sometimes she rolls out phrases and long speeches on a single note, without an inflection, lifting some phrases an octave higher. The charm then is almost solely in the extraordinary purity of the voice; it is a stream of gold without any dross or flaw. The charm is also in the *timbre*; one feels that this metal is living, that a soul vibrates in those resonances which are joined together like long waves. At other times, whilst keeping the same tone, this magician hammers her delivery, passes certain syllables through the rolling-mill of her teeth, and words fall upon one another like golden pieces. At certain moments, they fall at such a rate that one only hears their noise without understanding their meaning; this assuredly is a fault which my ecstatic prejudice cannot prevent me from recognizing. But often this monotonous and pure elocution, like that of a wearied idol which does not deign, as do common mortals, to spend its energies on useless and noisy inflections, has something that is elevated and charming. And this elocution is admirably suited to the calmer portions of the part of Féodora. There is something that is infinite and distant in this imperturbable and limpid chanting ; it seems, in truth, to come from the land of snows and boundless steppes.

On the whole, it is perhaps this artifice and the contrast which it makes with the passages in which the actress returns to a natural way of speaking, that constitute the originality of Madame Sarah Bernhardt's rendering. This recitative is doubtless to the spoken part what the strange and splendid costumes are to the acted part : it gives it a colour and savour of exoticism. Strange and true, both in a most surprising degree, Madame Sarah Bernhardt has besides a charm that cannot be analysed. I confess that I am one of her very pious admirers. We wish you, Madame, a pleasant journey, though we very much regret that you are leaving us for so long. You are going to show yourself over there, to men of little art and little literature, who will understand you badly, who will look at you with the same eye as people look at a calf with five legs, who will see in you a noisy and extravagant being, not the infinitely seductive artist, and who will only recognize that you have talent because they will pay a great deal to hear you. Endeavour to save your grace and to bring it back to us intact. For I hope that you will come back, though that America is very far away, and you have already borne more fatigues and gone through more adventures than the fabulous heroines of ancient romances. Come back then to the Comédie-Française and rest in the admiration and ardent sympathy of that good Parisian people who forgive you everything, as they owe you some of their greatest joys. Then, one fine evening, die suddenly on the stage, with a great tragic cry, for old age would be too harsh for you. And if you have time to collect yourself before you plunge into eternal night, bless, like M. Renan, the obscure First Cause. You have not perhaps been one of the most reasonable women of this century, but you shall have lived more than entire multitudes, and you shall have been one of the most graceful apparitions that have ever fluttered, for the consolation of men, over the changing surface of this world of phenomena.

MADAME DE SÉVIGNÉ

MADAME DE SÉVIGNÉ is the charming patroness of those who write for the newspapers.

This could be proved without asking too much from the facts. From the day on which she began to write, she knew that her letters were shown, copied, and collected ; in a word, that she had a public—a public composed, not of a hundred thousand daily readers, but of fifty or a hundred rich, noble, distinguished, cultivated, idle persons. What matter ? More or less consciously she wrote for this choice public, whence, little by little, comes a faint touch of the professional writer. She became a 'letter-writer,' that is to say, a journalist. She wrote accounts of the Court, of the town, of literature and the theatre, of provincial doings, of country doings, of watering places, of war, of celebrated crimes, of fashion, of family and personal matters—

accounts of everything that still finds a place in the newspapers. People quoted her *Letter about the Horse*, her *Letter about the Meadow*, her *Letter about the Death of Turenne*, her *Letter on the Death of Vatel*. And people asked one another : ' Have you read Madame de Sévigné's last letter ? ' just as under the Empire : ' Have you read Villemont's or Scholl's or Rochefort's last article ? '

She was ' natural,' of course. In other words she had naturally the warm, smart, excessive style, with too much movement, too many gestures, too much noise, that marks out the ' brilliant journalist.'

I will confess to you that this ' go ' often deafens and jostles against me ; I am anxious to be excused from it. But one cannot deny that she had a droll and powerful imagination. And then she knew her language.

At bottom she had a good heart, good sense, and a mind, I will not say average, but in exact harmony with her surroundings, and with almost nothing that outstripped them. I believe she was less intelligent than thê enigmatical Madame de Maintenon or the subtle and ironical Madame de La Fayette.

She brought up her daughter deplorably, guided her to worship herself, nurtured her with the most foolish ideas of greatness.

Her judgment was never independent or inventive. It goes without saying that she glorified the Revocation of the Edict of Nantes. For the executions in Brittany she had only a word of rapid pity and some prudent reflections. She was, indeed, faithful to Fouquet ; but not for a moment did this Christian woman appear to form for herself any real picture of the moral case of that man of finance. She followed in all their tastes and opinions the people of her world, of her coterie, or of her age. Like them she left off with La Calprenède ; she was for Corneille against Racine. She saw nothing superior to Nicole. She went ' to hear Bourdaloue ' because she liked him, but also because other people went. She never passed any judgment on the king, not the smallest ; and so on.

But she expresses common ideas and feelings with a most surprising vivacity and spirit. One feels an energy of temperament that was unable to find vent in other ways. And it is in this that Madame de Sévigné's life is curious—more so, perhaps, than her writings.

This jolly, expansive, lively, fair-haired woman, of passionate blood (you remember the sombre ardour of her grandmother Chantal, stepping over a son's body in order to enter the cloister), this over-healthy woman, a widow at twenty-six who evidently remained chaste, had for issue her letters—and Madame de Grignan.

Two peculiarities caused her maternal love to become truly the occupation of her whole life—she was not loved by her daughter, and she hardly ever saw her. And thus, on the one hand, the fear of displeasing her and the continual necessity of conquering her kept her love active ; and, on the other hand, the six hundred miles which separated her from that dry person allowed her to embellish her the more easily, to adore the image she had formed of her, and not to fall out with the model. Moreover it is certain that the ' fixed idea,' the obsessing representation of the idolized object, more fully exercises the powers of the soul than its real presence would do.

Madame de Sévigné left Marguerite in a

convent until she was eighteen years old, and
we know that, when mother and daughter
met, they could not understand one another.
It was not that Madame de Sévigné was not
profoundly sincere in her furious tenderness ;
but she needed, in order to display herself com-
fortably, the melancholy that absence leaves
and the illusion that it brings with it. Her
maternal love was thus a sort of half-tragic
' sport ' to which she devoted all her energies.

There is something of a gamble and of auto-
suggestion in the burning pages in which she
conveys this saint-worship. Madame de
Sévigné spent her life worshipping a Shadow
—like her grandmother Saint Chantal. And
that turned her aside from evil.

It is especially on this account that she is
interesting ; and it is on this account only
that this jovial creature suffered. Her com-
plaints were discreet, but all the more significant. ' The thought of not being loved
by you,' she once wrote, ' is not easy to
support, *believe me.*'

And whilst she wore herself out for the
pitiless pedant who did not love her, she did
not perceive that her son, Charles, for whom

she cared little, loved her with all his heart, and that he was a perfectly delightful boy.

This, in my opinion, was Madame de Sévigné's strange fate. Otherwise there is only one point in which she goes a little beyond the intellectual and emotional alignment of the people of her time. I mean her fondness for the country, another fruit of her enforced solitude as a widow. She loves nature and knows how to enjoy it as much as La Fontaine does; better than he, and by fresher combinations of words ('the singing leaves'), she renders its direct impression, that which immediately succeeds to the sensation. The ancestress of journalists, she is in some degree also that of the impressionist writers.

And, in conclusion, I beg you to be persuaded that I have a keen affection for this fat Mother Joy—who, at certain moments, was I believe also a mother of sorrow.

JOUBERT

SAINTE-BEUVE, and some others after him, discovered Joubert thirty [1] years ago. Then he was forgotten. But perhaps the moment has come to 'produce' him afresh. For do you know what Joubert is? An accomplished—and innocent Symbolist.

Moreover, he is an 'old original,' full of delightful eccentricities and angelic whims—who perhaps owed it to his poor digestion that he was an irreproachable and inventive idealist, a sort of sentimental dilettante. He knew d'Alembert, Diderot, and the Encyclopædists, and thought them shockingly vulgar. During the Revolution he lay hid in Villeneuve-sur-Yonne, a little Burgundy town, itself hidden in a smiling landscape, inhabited by good-humoured people, which, like most of the little towns and villages of

[1] 1880.

France, passed through the Revolution without noticing it. But the noise and spectacle of the Terror, although distant, finished detaching Joubert from this brutal world of bodily things.

He married late in life, and his marriage also was idealist. He espoused, out of admiration, a very pious, very unhappy, and very devoted old maid, of profound merit. Imagine —and it will be accurate in spite of the chronology—that he married Eugénie de Guérin.

Joubert was a great dangler after feminine souls. With Madame de Beaumont, Madame de Guitant, Madame de Lévis, Madame de Duras, and Madame de Vintmille, he had a tender and pure intercourse, more caressing than friendship, calmer than love. He was the more languid Doudan of two or three aristocratic little drawing-rooms which gathered in Paris at the beginning of the Empire, and in which, along with the old politeness, there reigned the most elegant religiosity. In them, with a thousand graces, one loved God and Chateaubriand.

Often ill, Joubert almost liked to be ill,

he felt that illness made his soul more subtle.
He had refinements in the style of des Esseintes (think of a des Esseintes who was
without perversity). He tore out of the books
of the eighteenth century those pages which
offended him, and retained only the innocent
pages in their almost empty bindings. He
adored perfumes, fruits, and flowers. He had
his own ways of regarding and recommending
the Catholic religion. ' The ceremonies of
Catholicism,' he wrote, ' incline to politeness.'

He did not hold truth in very great account ;
he preferred beauty ; or rather he confused
the two with a Seraphic astuteness. Do you
not think that Renan would have counter-
signed this thought : ' Endeavour to reason
broadly. It is not necessary that truth
should be found exactly in all the words,
provided it is in the thought and in the phrase.
It is, in fact, good that reason should have its
own beauty, and beauty is incompatible with
too rigid a precision.' And this : ' History
needs distance as its perspective. Facts and
events that are too well attested have, in a
fashion, ceased to be malleable.'

He is more of a Platonist than Plato. The

universe for him is a very exact system of symbols in which he endeavours to seize hold of the correspondences between the real and the ideal, the reflection of God in things. Where this reflection is lacking, he closes his eyes. He does not allow matter to exist only in so far as it is a representation of something spiritual. In itself it disgusts him. Accordingly, he reduces it as much as he can. He only admits that at the most it has the thickness of an onion-peel ; he regards the world as a prodigious piece of gold-beater's skin. This is literally the case. ' A grain of matter,' he says, ' has been enough to create the world. . . . This mass which frightens us is nothing more than a grain of matter which the Eternal has created and set to work. By its ductility, by the hollows which it holds, and by the Workman's art, it presents a sort of immensity in the decorations that have proceeded from it. . . . By taking back His own breath, the Creator could reduce its volume and easily destroy it.'

Like his metaphysics, his literary criticism is nothing but metaphors, comparisons, and allegories. He says of Voltaire : ' Voltaire, like a monkey, has charming movements and hideous features.' He says of Plato : ' Plato loses himself in the void, but one sees the play of his wings, one hears their noise.' He tells us that ' Xenophon writes with a pen made from a swan's feather, Plato with a pen of gold, and Thucydides with a stylet of bronze.' One is tempted to go on thus : ' Corneille writes with a pen made from an eagle's feather, Racine with one made from the feather of a turtle-dove (you know that the turtle-dove is violent), Chateaubriand with a pen made from a peacock's feather, Joubert himself with one made from the feather of an angel.

In politics he is for that form of government into which most artifice enters. What displeases him in democracy is that force and power finding themselves in the same hands, that is to say in those of the greatest number, ' there is no art, no equilibrium and political beauty.' He wants power to be separated from material force and from number, and to hold them in check. It is in this fiction that he sees beauty : ' Fiction is wanted everywhere. Even politics are a sort of poetry.'

His psychology is also made up of images. He remarks that man *lives* only in his head and his heart ; that language is a *cord* and speech an *arrow* ; that the soul is a *lighted vapour* of which the body is the *torch* ; that certain souls have no *wings*, nor even *feet* for stability, nor hands for work ; that the mind is the *atmosphere* of the soul, that it is a *fire* whose thought is the *flame* ; that imagination is the *eye* of the soul. Farther on, I see that the mind, which just now was an atmosphere and a flame, is a *field*, and then a *metal* ; that it can be *hollow* and *sonorous*, or that its *solidity* can be *plane*, so that thought produces on it the effect of the *blow of a hammer* ; then that it resembles a *concave* or a *convex* mirror ; that it is *cold*, that it is *warm* ; that modesty is a *net-work*, a *piece of velvet*, a *cocoon*, etc., etc.

Do you feel nature's revenge. This, for a despiser of matter, is a very material imagination. It' is the same with all those over-fastidious persons.

With all this, Joubert is very ' special.' His quintessential subtleties, his virginal Epicureanism, and what I call his ' angelicism ' can still give us, here and there, rather pleasant little throbs of the soul. By a thousand mysterious affectations, by his elaborate and delicious bad taste, he remains close to us. This modest sensitive writer is one of the most distinguished of those prettily whimsical artists who are, as it were, on the margin of literatures.

Only I ought to confess that Joubert always indicates both terms of his comparisons ; and it is this, among other things, which distinguishes him from, for instance, M. Stéphane Mallarmé. That does not prevent the relationship from existing. I wished to show our Symbolist poets that they have an unexpected but authentic ancestor.

VIRGIL

Assuredly Virgil, among the great poets, is one of those who have had the most luck.

There are three famous phrases that have a very fine meaning, and that by being continually quoted, keep his memory in an eternal spring-time.

First, there is the Sibylline verse :

' Magnus ab integro sæclorum nascitur ordo.'

' A new era begins.' (It is usual to mangle the text and to say : ' Novus rerum nascitur ordo.') As Virgil happened to write this and the following verses about the time of the birth of Christ, the Middle Ages declared him to be a Christian, a prophet, and a magician. Lettered monks prayed for his soul. Dante chose him as his guide in the other world as far as the threshold of Paradise. And Victor Hugo wrote :

' Dans Virgile parfois, dieu tout près d'être un ange,
Le vers porte à sa cime une lueur étrange.
C'est que, rêvant déjà ce qu'à présent on sait,
Il chantait presque à l'heure où Jésus vagissait. . .
Dieu voulait qu'avant tout, rayon du Fils de l'homme,
L'aube de Bethléem blanchit le front de Rome.' [1]

Then there is the inevitable ' Sunt lacrymæ rerum.' Since the time of the romantics it has been bravely translated by ' Things themselves have tears.' Or, in Hugo's style, ' The tears of things, these exist.' And the hemistich is compared with Lamartine's verse :

' Objets inanimés, avez-vous donc une âme ? ' [2]

And it is affirmed with an appearance of reason that all the poetry of the nineteenth century exists in germ in these three words of the pious Æneas.

Lastly, Virgil has said : ' We weary of all things except of understanding.' An admirable phrase, worthy of Sainte-Beuve or of Renan, and one which seems to be the proper

---

[1] ' Sometimes in Virgil, that god who is almost an angel, the verse bears a strange light on its summit. The reason is that, already dreaming of what is now known, he sang almost at the hour when Jesus was wailing as a child. . . . God wished that a ray of the Son of Man, the dawn from Bethlehem, should first gleam upon the brow of Rome.'

[2] ' Inanimate objects, have you then a soul ? '

device for dilettantism or even for philosophy. Virgil was thus ignorant of none of the great theories of his time, which are also plainly those of our own. Old Anchises speaks like a good Pantheist in the sixth book of the *Æneid*, and Silenus, in the sixth *Eclogue* appears to be imbued with the doctrine of evolution.

Thus Christianity and all poetry and all philosophy are contained in a few of Virgil's words, like a field of roses in a phial, the noise of the ocean in a shell, or the sky in a drop of water.

Now, the "magnus sæclorum nascitur ordo" is only one of the agreeably hyperbolical touches in an occasional piece, a ' compliment' of welcome to the newly-born child of a rich protector, Asinius Pollio. It is hardly necessary to recall the fact that the ' tears of things ' is a radical mistranslation. When Æneas, seeing some paintings which represent the siege of Troy in the temple of Venus at Carthage, makes the remark, ' Sunt lacrymæ rerum,' it simply means, as you know : ' Our sad renown has then reached this country ! *Our misfortunes obtain tears here*, and there is

pity here for human destiny.' And, finally,
the profound utterance, ' We weary of all
things except of understanding,' is not in
Virgil's works, but is only attributed to him
by the commentator, Servius.

Whence it follows that the most living part
of his fame is founded on a false meaning, on a
mistranslation and an uncertain tradition.

I hasten to add that Virgil deserves this
strange fortune, and that never was an error
more intelligent than that which benefits such
a poet. For all his work gives, in the highest
degree, the idea of a great mind and, at
the same time, of a melancholy and tender
soul.

Graceful, vigorous, or tragic images rise
from his poems and remain in our memories
long after we no longer read him. There are
in the *Eclogues* the gentle exile, Melibœus,
and, no matter what I may have said, the
radiant cradle of the redeeming child, and the
earth agitated with a divine hope. There are
in the *Georgics* the hymn of Jupiter and of
Cybele, the sacred intoxication of spring, the
brotherhood of plants, animals, and men, the
serenity and beneficence of rural life—and the

despair of the symbolical Orpheus, of the eternal Orpheus weeping for the eternal Eurydice. There is in the *Æneid* the love of the Tyrian Dido, the most ardent and the most tortured of women of thirty years of age ; the red light of her funeral pyre on the sea, and the silent flight of her phantom in the pale Elysian myrtles. There is Hector's Andromache kneeling by an empty tomb, preserving a single love and fidelity of heart in the involuntary infidelity of a slave's body ; the loving friendship of Nisus and Euryalus ; Pallas, or the grace of youth cut off ; the fair Amazon Camilla, the young ancestress of all heroic ' disguised women ' from Clorinda to Joan of Arc, and there is everywhere the shadow of the great Wolf, the majesty of the Roman people, rulers and pacifiers of the world, the feeling of their mission, of their earthly ' vocation,' believed in and revered like a religious dogma : ' Excudent alii.'

All this is crowded together, condensed into chosen expressions of a profoundly significant brevity, which prolong themselves and resound in the heart and the imagination. No one has written verses more fully charged with soul, and it is true that all this forms only some hundreds of verses.

The remainder. . . . Oh ! the remainder is the acme of art, and·even of artifice. Nothing is less spontaneous. Virgil is the first of the poets of the study. He appropriates and combines Homer, Hesiod, the Greek tragedians, Apollonius, Theocritus, and Lucretius, in what were formerly called industrious larcenies. He was an official poet, a Poet Laureate, a Tennyson.

The *Æneid* is a miracle of ingenuity, an extraordinary feat of skill. It is a national poem, written in faith, but to order. Its programme was a difficult one. It was necessary to insert into the narrative the whole of epic Rome, the history of Rome from its beginning to the battle of Actium, the legend of the old races who had first peopled the Latin soil, a sort of directory of the nobility who claimed that they were the issue of the companions of Æneas ; the whole Roman religion, the indigenous gods, the manners and public and private usages of the Roman people, etc. Virgil succeeded in doing this. The *Æneid* is a masterpiece of mosaic, executed by the most patient of the poets who wrote Alexandrine verses.

Virgil spent thirty years composing the twelve thousand verses which he has left us. In the parts of his work that are least read his poetry is marvellously picturesque and plastic. That of M. Leconte de Lisle and M. de Heredia resembles it closely.

What is tender seems to be more tender, what is moving more moving, what is human more human, what is simple more simple, in poetry so learned and composite as this. Sometimes, in the episodes, tears change into precious stones. We are more touched when, among those hard Virgilian gems, a jewel stirs, trembles, lives, is a tear, and makes us remember that this official poet, this Poet Laureate, this King of Parnassians, deserves by his sweetness to be called ' the young girl.

THE AUTHOR OF 'THE IMITATION'

HE is fashionable. To quote him is the vogue. Do we really like him? And why do we like him? Is his ideal, which is composed of chastity, poverty, and obedience, is it ours? What is there in common between this fourteenth century ascetic and ourselves? Let us try and find out.

In the first place, he pleases us by the perfect picture which he suggests to us, to us who are so rushed, of a recluse and silent life, the life of which we sometimes dream, of a pure and white retreat in the midst of this hell of earth, still sweeter to think of in the century of the Jacqueries and of the Hundred Years' War.

Then it amuses us to discover here and there in his anonymous book a little of his own life and personality. I even prefer to know him only through his book. It was a time when

Churchmen burnt heretics and sorcerers for the glory of God, and I would be afraid to learn something about him that might grieve me. He was not a member of a rigorously cloistered order. ' It is commendable in a religious person,' he says, ' seldom to go abroad.' Thus he could go abroad. ' Be not familiar with any woman ; but commend all good women in general to God.' Thus he was acquainted with women. He was not an Abbot or a Prior, and he held no great ecclesiastical office. ' My son,' says Jesus Christ to him, ' trouble not thyself if thou seest others honoured and advanced, whilst thou art contemned and abased. . . . To others this or that shall be committed, but thou shalt be accounted a thing of no use. At this nature will sometimes be troubled, and it is a great thing if thou bear it in silence.'

He had studied metaphysics, and he had abandoned the study : ' What need have we to concern ourselves with *genera* and *species* ? ' He had plunged into profane letters, and these he never quite abandoned. I like to think that he prayed for Virgil's soul. He, the saint, quotes Seneca, the philosopher ; he, the ascetic, quotes Ovid. It is true that he does not name them out of a pious shame.

Whatever he does, he remains devoted to beauty, even to human beauty. He writes very well, with elegance, often with more elegance than is necessary, that is to say, with polish. God forgive him, but he has much more care for rhetorical rules than had Christ on the mountain. He loves antithesis, parallelism in his constructions, assonance, alliteration. His prose is full of symmetrical constructions, is almost always rhythmical, and often rhymed : 'Amor modum sæpe necessit, sed super omnem modum fervescit. . . .' 'Amor vigilat, et dormiens non dormitat. Fatigatus non lassatur, arctatus non coarctatur, territus non conturbatur.'[1]

He is sensitive to beautiful landscapes, interested in the charming or magnificent forms of the earth, and he blamed himself for it : 'What canst thou see anywhere which thou canst not see where thou art ? Behold the heaven and the earth and all the elements ;

[1] 'Love knoweth no bounds, but is fervent beyond measure. . . .' 'Love watcheth, and, sleeping, slumbereth not. Though weary, it is not tired, though pressed, it is not straitened ; though alarmed, it is not confounded.'

for of these are all things created.' It was doubtless during a sunset in summer, at the hour when, to speak like Hugo, ' an immense goodness fills the firmament,' that in a mood of tenderness he wrote: ' There is no creature so small and abject that it representeth not the goodness of God.' And perhaps, re-assured by this thought, he permitted himself for once to admire without scruple this un-restrained, unmortified Pagan Nature, which is not cloistered, which is not chaste, which loves life, and which does not pray except in the verses of the poets.

He pleases us also by the contrast that exists between his own profound gentleness and the pitiless austerity of his doctrine, and by the manner in which he accommodates his very human soul to an inhuman ideal. This distant monk whose words are stern and whose voice is tender, makes one think of those emaciated figures in Gothic windows, those figures whose lines are stiff and whose colour is pleasing, and whose rigid contours are bathed in a beautiful mysterious light.

His doctrine is the complete renunciation of every natural feeling, even of those that are regarded as noble and generous earthly affections, knowledge, intellectual ambitions, in a word, everything which does not help towards 'salvation.' He has a quantity of horrible maxims, for instance : ' Neither desire that the heart of any should be set on thee, nor do thou set thy heart on the love of any.' Nothing is more bitter than his counsels of detachment, but nothing is more loving than his conversations with Jesus.

Now he who thus loves God, loves men. What does it matter if this love does not rest on us, and if it is from God that it descends again upon us ? Plato had already said, like the author of *The Imitation*, or almost like him, that ' love tends always upwards, because love is born of God, and it can find rest only in God.' Read again in the *Banquet* the story of that perpetual and necessary ascent of love, which always outstrips finite beings in order to mount higher, either to a personal God or to what has been called, from lack of another word, the ' category of the Ideal.' We always love in some fashion beyond those whom we love. He had indeed the heart of a man, a gentle and tender heart, that monk who

wrote : ' He doeth much that loveth much.
He doeth much that doeth a thing well. He
doeth well that rather serveth the common
weal than his own will. . . . No man is
without fault ; no man but hath his burden ;
no man is sufficient of himself ; no man is wise
enough of himself ; but we ought to bear with
one another, comfort one another, help,
instruct, and admonish one another.'

And then, in spite of everything, there is
even in the extreme maxims of ascetic detachment a point in which they remain human.
Among the things that they reprove, there are
some from which we like people to be detached,
and from which it pleases us to appear to be
detached. While asceticism runs counter to
several of our natural feelings, at the same
time it flatters our instincts for justice and our
revolts against the world as it is. The ascetic
is less unwelcome in putting our affections and
our pleasures under his feet when we see him
treating the causes of our sufferings in the
same way. We have a weakness for the
plebeian saints who speak ill of the rich, the
powerful, the happy people of this world.
And the saints themselves are doubtless not

displeased to be able with a secure conscience
to despise what the vulgar detest from a
natural inclination. Here, at least, nature
and grace are in accord.

It is certain, lastly, that if this detachment
snatches away our pleasures from us, it also
frees us from our servitudes. It satisfies in us
the desire for liberty, for independence in
regard to things, for supremacy over all that is
subject to the laws of chance and brutal force.
The ascetic trembles with joy at no longer
feeling himself bound to things, to men, to
events, at seeing nothing except on high :
' He that careth not to please men, nor feareth
to displease them, shall enjoy much peace. . . .
Who is more free than he who desireth nothing
on earth ? '

I asked myself what there is in common
between this saint and ourselves. There are
his negations, and there is his melancholy.
Pessimism is the half of saintliness ; in *The
Imitation* it is this half which makes us
indulgent to the other. We seek in it for the
means, not of sanctifying ourselves, but of
pacifying ourselves ; not a cordial, but an
anodyne, a *nepenthe* ; not the red rose of

divine love, but the pale lotus blossom which is the flower of forgetfulness. I have always wished to give to this little book as a symbolical epigraph De Quincey's phrase : ' Oh ! just, subtle, and mighty opium, thou hast the keys of Paradise.' We take as the end of our journey the point from which this pious solitary started. We learn from him, even to-day, not to live ·in God, but to live in ourselves, and in such a way as not to suffer men.